A Pastor and Ministry Director

Six or seven years ago, I attended an event called "The Battle" that was part of a program that Irv Woolf started called "Every Man's Battle For Purity". That day led me to being a part of a Purity Boot Camp for a week, then a Purity Platoon for six months and ultimately building a strong and deeply accountable friendship with a fellow pastor whom I've met with once a week ever since. "The Power of Purity" captures the core teachings and practices promoted in the "Every Man's Battle For Purity" ministry. This ministry has lifted my soul, taken me out of an isolated struggle with sin, strengthened me in spiritual battle and blessed my life immensely. We live in a culture saturated with sex. Every man has access to immoral, addicting images at a push of a button on his computer at any time. Because of that, Christian men, in mass, are sinking into lives filled with pornography - typically lived in isolation and lack of accountability. Purity is vital. Sin is epidemic. And this book gives powerful tools to liberate both men and women from the bonds of sexual sin. I highly recommend it.

Dan Adler
Director, Heart of the City Ministries

foxes Book of Martyrs

i

A Theologian

God created us as sexual beings and intended sex to be a means for procreation and for intimate pleasure between husband and wife. When separated from God, sex has become a means for exploitation, addiction, and enslavement. Irv Woolf is a godly pastor who has helped many find their freedom in Christ by overcoming enslavement to sexual sins and addictions. I pray that many will read this powerful book on sexual purity.

Dr. Neil T. Anderson
Founder and President Emeritus of Freedom in Christ Ministries
Author, *Winning The Battle Within*

A Marriage and Family Therapist

This is a unique and long-overdue book that EVERY man will find valuable. Irv knows the Bible, knows men, knows what it's like to live in the real world and knows how to help men enjoy the healthy sexuality that God designed us to experience and enjoy. Paul tells us to "guard our heart" and Irv shows us simple and practical ways that men living in a sex-saturated 21st century can do just that. Irv helps us understand that purity is the greatest pathway to the kinds of pleasure that every man desires. If you want a practical, relevant, honest, explicit, Biblically-based, psychologically sound resource to help you both cultivate healthy sexuality, protect and encourage your heart then read this book.

Dr. Gary J. Oliver
Executive Director of The Center for Relationship Enrichment
Professor of Psychology and Practical Theology, John Brown University
Author, *Mad About Us: Moving from Anger to Intimacy With Your Spouse*

THE POWER OF

PURITY

GOD'S DESIGN FOR SEX IN A

SEX-SATURATED WORLD

Irv Woolf

Forward by Dr. Mark Laaser

THE POWER OF PURITY:

GOD'S DESIGN FOR SEX IN A

SEX-SATURATED WORLD

Copyright © 2009 Dr. Irving A. Woolf

ISBN: 978-0-578-01918-5

Published by:
Hopewell Publishing
A division of Hopewell Marriage & Family Institute
P. O. Box 631
Osseo, MN 55369

Printed by:
Bethany Press
6820 West 115th Street
Bloomington MN 55438

www.bethanypress.com

Dedication

Lovingly dedicated to my bride, Elsie,

who consistently reflects the purity of the Bride of Christ.

Let us rejoice and be glad and give him glory! For the wedding

of the Lamb has come, and his bride has made herself ready.

Fine linen, bright and clean, was given her to wear." (Fine linen

stands for the righteous acts of the saints.)

Revelation 19:7–8

ACKNOWLEDGEMENTS

This book began in response to a course on addictions I took at Denver Seminary in 2001. As part of the course, I was assigned to write a paper on sexual addiction and describe what a three-year program of sexual purity would look like in the congregation in which I pastored. I had a particular interest in the subject since I had struggled with sexual sin for most of my life. This was the chance to learn about the roots of sexual addiction. Little did I know that God would use the course I took in the summer of 2001 to change my life. As Jesus said in Luke 4:23, "Physician, heal thyself," that course caused me to work on healing myself. It forced me to do a lot of soul-searching and self-examination. It led me to confront my own sins and gain my own healing before I could address the needs of others. As part of my healing, I worked through the text and workbook, *Faithful and True,* by Mark Laaser. It was an eye-opening and cathartic experience. It produced a passion in me for sexual purity and for the purity of the Bride of Christ. That passion has never waned and I find myself as committed to seeing Christ's Bride, the Church, become sexually pure as I was when I first took that course in 2001.

I want to express my deep appreciation to a number of people who have contributed to the writing of this book. The first on my list is my wife, Elsie, who has been my most ardent supporter and "cheerleader." She loves Jesus Christ and me, in that order. Her belief in the purity of the Bride is unparalleled. She co-authored chapter seven of this book, "The Power of a Pure Woman."

I would also like to thank my mentor and friend, Dr. Mark Laaser. Mark encouraged me to develop Every Man's Battle For Purity, as a men's ministry for the local church. His helpful suggestions and wise guidance have proven invaluable.

I want to thank the many men, women, and teens who have been through the purity ministries offered by our organization, the National Coalition For Purity. They provided the "field testing" for much of what is described in this book. They have taught me what works and what doesn't work when it comes to helping men become sexually pure. They have taught me how men think and behave, their interests and peculiarities. I thank them all. They have changed my life and shaped the ministry.

I want to thank three pastors at New Hope Church. Pastor Stephen Paul Goold, Senior Pastor of New Hope Church, like Dr. Laaser, believed in me and supported the purity ministry. He instinctively knew that the church would benefit from it. I also want to thank Pastors David Rodquist and Timothy Brannagan. Both men "jumped into the deep end of the pool" with me when Every Man's Battle For Purity was first launched in 2002. They received "battle field promotions" and were made sergeants of the first purity platoons. They led their platoons with honor and effectiveness.

I want to thank those who have proofread, edited, and offered suggestions. My thanks to Carolyn Lung, who has gone home to be with the Lord. Carolyn was a long-time friend, ministry partner, and one of the most talented ladies I have ever known. I would also like to thank Stefanie Grundahl, Lisa Dorau, and Melissa Southard for their able administrative work on this material during my years as a staff pastor at New Hope Church (formerly Crystal Evangelical Free Church) in New Hope, Minnesota. I want to thank Beryl Henne who edited the manuscript from her home in Winnipeg, Canada. I also want to acknowledge Amy Printy who faithfully leads our e-mail prayer team. Amy and the team of prayer warriors have bathed this book in prayer since its inception. My thanks to Brian Lund for his excellent work on the layout of the book, Kristyn Goold for her creative cover design, and Sara Rosenberg and all of those at Bethany Press who worked on this "labor of love."

Finally, I would be remiss if I didn't thank the Lord Jesus Christ who gave me the vision, desire, and passion for this ministry. My first response to His still small voice was the same as Moses', "O Lord, please send someone else to do it" (Exod. 4:13). The task seemed too overwhelming and too shameful. God has helped me heal and persuaded me that He never calls us to do what He does not also enable. Now my testimony is that "by the grace of God I am what I am, and his grace to me was not without effect" (1 Cor. 15:10).

Table of Contents

FORWARD

It doesn't take a lot to recognize that we live in a highly sexualized culture. Billboards and store fronts use sexual messages to call us to buy their products or services. Magazines and newspapers assault us with sexual ads. Turn on the television, computer, and, specifically, the internet and the sexuality becomes even more blatant often crossing the line into pornography. Sexual messages showing an abundance of skin are used to sell everything from lingerie to beer. As if that wasn't enough, there are advertisements for erectile dysfunction, penile enlargement, breast augmentation, and all manner of birth control on television, radio, and in print. People have become numb to the boldness of these messages and no longer blush. We are boiling in a sexual stew and like the proverbial frog in the kettle, we are being cooked as the heat rises and society's standards are lowered.

Are Christians immune from all of this? Were that it was so! Christian men, women, and teens are called to be "in the world, not of it." (Romans 12:2) Yet, by being in the world, many have become conformed to the world. Instead of serving as thermostats and changing the culture, many have become thermometers reflecting the culture in which they live.

The culture uses sexuality in ways never intended by God. As the poster picturing gears, chains, sprockets, and wheels all tightly strung together wistfully muses, "God made us plain and simple. My how we have complicated things." God designed sex to be plain and simple. His original design was for sex to be for procreation and pleasure. His original design was for men and women to use sex to carry out His command to "be fruitful and multiply; fill the earth" (Genesis 1:28). Sex is to be the glue of marriage sealing the marital covenant between a husband and wife.

Irv Woolf takes us back to that original blueprint, back to sex as God originally intended it. Irv shows us the clear difference sexual purity makes in the life of a man, a woman, a marriage, and a family. He describes how the world, the flesh, and the devil have corkscrewed sexuality and twisted it into a self-serving distortion of what God intended it to be. I have known Irv since we first met in 2001 at Denver Seminary where I taught a Doctor of Ministry class on addictions. Irv is no ivory tower theologian but a man who applies the Word of God in practical fashion to the everyday world of temptations. He understands what it takes to live in purity. As a former pastor who launched Every Man's Battle For Purity in his home church, Irv is eminently qualified to write about this topic. God's hand is upon him and his ministry to purify the Bride of Christ. May the Lord use him. The Church desperately needs purifying.

Mark Laaser, Ph.D
Eden Prairie, Minnesota
Director, Faithful and True Ministries
Author, *Healing the Wounds of Sexual Addiction*
www.faithfulandtrueministries.com

CHAPTER ONE
INTRODUCTION

With a mighty voice he shouted: "Fallen! Fallen is Babylon the Great! ... For all the nations have drunk the maddening wine of her adulteries. The kings of the earth committed adultery with her, and the merchants of the earth grew rich from her excessive luxuries."

Revelation 18:2–3

The Tsunami of Sexual Immorality

The Internet is like a large city that never sleeps. In this city are shopping malls with stores of every conceivable type, art galleries, libraries, museums, and sports pavilions. There are restaurants, stock exchanges, schools, and hospitals. The city also has a disproportionately large "red light" district that takes up nearly 12 percent of the city. In this red light district there is pornography, sexual chat rooms, and real-time sexual videos. Prostitutes ply their trade, and pedophiles stalk their victims in this part of town.

The Internet is like a large city, and just like any large city, it is both a blessing and a curse. The Internet has provided people with technological access to unparalleled volumes of information, ease and speed in business transactions, and worldwide connectedness. Missionaries on the other side of the world can report ministry needs, prayer requests, triumphs, and defeats

15

in a matter of moments. All of these are the blessings of the Internet. The downside, the curse side of the Internet, is that it has also ushered in an era of instant access to pornography and all manner of sexual perversions.

Forty years ago if a man wanted to look at pornography, he sent away to France and it was mailed to him in a plain brown wrapper. It was all so secretive and taboo. Prior to the advent of Playboy forty years ago, the crudest magazine in America was Esquire, a man's magazine that occasionally featured line drawings of naked women. Today, pornography is accessible through television, cable and satellite television, magazines, DVDs, videos, books, cell phones, peep shows, strip clubs, PDAs, and the Internet. Today all anyone need do to access the crudest pornography imaginable is turn on the computer in their home office. No longer do they need to drive to an adult bookstore to find pornography. The Internet has become an accelerant for spreading sexual immorality.

Sexual Immorality is a Worldwide Problem

The Bible exhorts us to "flee from sexual immorality ..." (1 Cor. 6:18). We have not heeded God's exhortation. Sexual immorality is a vast and growing problem costing billions of dollars not only in the United States but worldwide. Because of the swift growth of the sex industry, statistics become quickly outdated. However, to provide the reader with some idea of how extensive this industry is, the Web site, Internet Filter Review, says that in 2006, 97.06 billion dollars was spent worldwide on pornography alone and 13.33 billion dollars in the United States. The revenues from pornography are larger than the combined revenues of all professional sports franchises in the United States and the combined revenues of the three major television networks ABC, CBS, and NBC. Forty million adults in the United

States, both men and women, regularly visit Internet pornography Web sites. Disappointingly, 47 percent of Christians said that pornography is a major problem in their homes. One of three visitors to all adult Web sites is a woman. The Internet Filter Review Web site adds that, "Women, far more than men, are likely to act out their behaviors in real life, such as having multiple partners, casual sex, or affairs."[1]

Based upon the above statistics, the United States ranks fourth in per capita dollars spent on pornography. Countries in the Far East rank in the top three. However, the Internet Filter Review statistics also indicate that the United States is the leading exporter of pornography to the world. It is one of our chief national exports, although that fact is seldom acknowledged. Is the United States "Babylon the Great," the harlot? Without rushing to judgment, the parallels between the United States and the great harlot of the end times are striking indeed. The book of Revelation says Babylon the Great is one with whom "all the nations have drunk the maddening wine of her adulteries. The kings of the earth committed adultery with her, and the merchants of the earth grew rich from her excessive luxuries" (Rev. 18:3). Rather than "adulteries," a more accurate translation of the Greek word is "sexual immorality."[2] The nations become drunk on her sexual immorality.

Stages of Sexual Immorality

Sexual immorality is much more than pornography. Sexual immorality spans the continuum from lust-filled stares at one end to criminal sexual behavior at the other. According to Patrick Carnes, sexual immorality

---

[1] Internet Filter Review, *Internet Pornography Statistics*, Retrieved August 11, 2007, from http://www.internetfilterreview.com/internet-pornography-statistics.html.

[2] μοιχείας [*moicheias*], "adultery," πορνείας [*porneias*], "sexual immorality."

may be categorized in three levels of sexually immoral behaviors:

(a) level one sexual immorality includes viewing pornography, affairs, prostitution, strip clubs, masturbation, and anonymous sex

(b) level two behaviors include exhibitionism, voyeurism, voyeur-exhibitionism, indecent calls, and liberties taken

(c) level three sexual immorality involves child molestation, rape, and incest

Each level becomes progressively more involved with others and more destructive.[3]

In the Sexual Interaction Table, Carnes' three-stage model has been modified to include a fourth stage that helps to distinguish between non-personal and anonymous sexual interaction. All four types of sexual interactions are sinful and immoral, some are illegal. All four types can be addictive. The four types move progressively from legal to illegal, from non-personal to personal, from anonymous to known, from low disease risk to high disease risk, and from consensual to non-consensual. Type A interactions do not involve another person. Examples of type A interactions would include pornography of all types and masturbation. Type A interactions are legal but can easily become addictive and are often "gateway" interactions leading to progressively more destructive sexual behaviors. Type B interactions are also legal, involve another person or persons, are consensual but are anonymous. Some examples of type B interactions would be sexual talk in Internet chat rooms, telephone sex, or sexual e-mail talk using pseudonyms. Type C interactions involve consensual physical contact with another person

---

[3] Patrick Carnes, *Out of the Shadows: Understanding Sexual Addiction* (Center City, MN: Hazelden, 2001), pp. 33–66.

or persons and may or may not be legal. Examples of type C include affairs, prostitution, and sexual clubs. Type D interactions involve non-consensual contact with another person or persons and are always illegal. Some examples of type D interactions are rape, incest, voyeurism, exhibitionism, and sexual harassment at work.

Sexual Interaction Table

	Type A	Type B	Type C	Type D
Nature of Interaction	Non-personal	Person to person, Anonymous and Consensual	Person to person, Consensual	Person to person Non-consensual
Description of Interaction	Behaviors that do not directly involve a second person	Involves a second person; however, both parties never meet person to person and purposely maintain anonymity	Involves the physical presence of a second person, the behavior is consensual and either party can be identified	Involves the physical presence of a second person, and the behavior is coerced or forced. The other person is known or unknown.
Legality of Interaction	Legal	Legal	Possibly illegal	Illegal
Disease Risk of Interaction (STDs)	None	None	High	High
Examples of Interaction	Masturbation, pornographic media: print, video, digital, computer	Telephone sex discussions, Internet chat rooms with sexual discussions, virtual sex	Sexually explicit performances, sexual intercourse, sexual touch, prostitution	Overt sexual harassment, rape, incest, molestation, exhibitionism

Sexual Immorality Is Not the Same as Sexual Addiction

Is sexual immorality the same as sexual addiction? No. Sexual immorality (*porneia*) includes all manner of sexual sin. All sexual addicts are sexual sinners, but not all sexual sinners are sexual addicts. The sexuality continuum moves from sexual temptation to sexual sin to sexual addiction.

Sexuality Continuum

Sexual Temptation	Sexual Sin	Sexual Addiction

To be sexually tempted is not a sin. Sexual temptation is a solicitation to sin. The Bible calls Satan "the tempter" who appeals to our flesh enticing us to sin (Matt. 4:3, 1 Thess. 3:5, James 1:13–15). Even Jesus was subject to the tempter's enticement to sexually sin, for the Bible says Jesus "has been tempted in every way, just as we are—yet was without sin" (Heb. 4:15). "Tempted in every way" has to include sexual temptation. So to be sexually tempted is not a sin.

Sexual sin is not sexual addiction. All of us are sinners, says Romans 3:23, and all of us sin in thought, word, deed, or attitude (1 John 1:8). The Bible teaches that as long as Christians are alive in the flesh, they face an internal conflict between the flesh and the spirit (Rom. 7:23). We continually face the choice to live righteously in obedience to God or to live sinfully, disobediently, and independently from God. The apostle John exhorts believers not to sin but should we sin, we have an advocate with the heavenly Father in Jesus Christ. He is the Christian's eternal propitiation for sin (1 John 2:1–2).

Sexual sin does not move into the category of sexual addiction until the sinful sexual behavior becomes ingrained, habitual, and the sinner cannot stop the behavior. The sexual sin has become uncontrollable. The term *sexual addict* in this book is used in a non-pejorative way recognizing that all sexual addicts are image-bearers of God who are under the mastery of their sexual sin and in bondage to it. However, for the sake of consistency and ease of understanding, the term *sexual addict* is employed. Sexual addicts vow, pray, and try hard to quit but find themselves returning to their sinful sexual behaviors like "a dog returns to its vomit" (Prov. 26:11). From the Bible's perspective, sexual addiction, like any addiction, is a form of bondage or slavery. Sexual sin has become the master and the sinner its slave. Under the inspiration of the Holy Spirit, the apostle Peter accurately describes the slavery of modern sexual addiction when he writes, "They promise them freedom, while they themselves are slaves of depravity—for a man is a slave to whatever has mastered him" (2 Pet. 2:19). Sexual temptation, like the unrighteous of Peter's day, promises sexual freedom but delivers sexual slavery.

According to Mark Laaser, "Sexual addiction is a sickness involving any type of uncontrollable sexual activity."[4] Harry Schaumberg states, "Sexual addiction is the term commonly used to describe sexual obsession. A sex addict is willing to be destructive to self and others, even breaking the law if necessary, to achieve sexual pleasure."[5] Further, Schaumburg affirms the words of Laaser, Carnes, and others when he writes, "Simply put, a person demonstrates sexually addictive behavior when he or she is preoccupied with a mood-altering experience in which sexual behaviors have become

[4] Mark Laaser, *Healing the Wounds of Sexual Addiction* (Grand Rapids, MI: Zondervan Publishing House, 2004), p. 23.
[5] Harry Schaumburg, *False Intimacy: Understanding the Struggle of Sexual Addiction* (Colorado Springs, CO: NavPress, 1997), p. 20.

uncontrollable regardless of the consequences to health, family and/or career."[6] The key word in the definitions of both Laaser and Schaumburg is "uncontrollable." For sexual addicts, unlike sexual sinners, the sinful sexual behavior has become uncontrollable. The addiction is master, the addict its slave. More than a physical or emotional disease, the roots of sexual addiction are spiritual. Sexual addiction is nothing less than spiritual idolatry of the heart. The sexual sin has become god in the addict's life.

Sexual Immorality Is a Problem for the Church of Jesus Christ

As noted in the Internet Filter Review Web site statistics previously cited, the problem of sexual immorality has invaded the church. According to The Barna Group (The Barna Group, 2004), the statistics for born-again Christians viewing porn, having adulterous affairs, becoming

> **"...the statistics for born-again Christians viewing porn, having adulterous affairs, becoming enslaved to sexual sin, cohabiting, and initiating divorces are virtually indistinguishable from those of the unsaved world."**

enslaved to sexual sin, cohabiting, and initiating divorces are virtually indistinguishable from those of the unsaved world.[7] John White draws the sobering conclusion that "the sexual behavior of Christians has reached the point of being indistinguishable from that of non-Christians ... in our sexual

---

6 Ibid., p. 22.
7 The Barna Group, *Faith has a Limited Effect on Most People's Behavior* (May 24, 2004), Retrieved August 11, 2007, from The Barna Group: http://www.barna.org/FlexPage.aspx?Page=BarnaUpdate&BarnaUpdateID=164.

behavior we, as a Christian community, are both in the world, and of it."[8]
The implications of this for the church are serious. Christian men and women
who engage in sexual immorality are living duplicitous, hypocritical lives
characterized by shame and silence. Because of this dualism, their spiritual
lives are shallow, impotent, and disengaged from the community of faith. To
the degree that this happens, the church is weakened and is not a threat to the
"gates of hell" (Matt. 16: 18 KJV). Randy Alcorn challenges the church when
he writes:

> In a climate of holiness, sin is hated—not tolerated, minimized,
> winked at, ignored, or mildly dismissed (Ps. 45:7; 97:10;
> 119:104; Prov. 8:13; 13:5; Rom. 12:9). In a climate of holiness
> the Gospel is seen not as a call to happiness but to holiness. This
> kind of wholehearted commitment is as contagious in a church
> as is moral laxity.[9]

How can the church be changed? To answer that question, we must
first answer a more basic question, "How can pastors, who lead the church, be
changed?" The three most common responses from pastors when challenged
to launch a purity ministry in their churches are:

(a) Denial. For many pastors the subject of sex is threatening.
Because sex is uncomfortable or embarrassing to talk about, their approach
is to deny that their congregations have a problem in the area of sexual sin or
sexual addiction. One pastor of a large church in the Minneapolis metroplex
told me, "You must have a lot of sexual sinners in your church. I don't have

---

[8] John White, *Flirting with the World* (Wheaton, IL: Harold Shaw Publishers,
1982), pp. 75, 81.
[9] Randy Alcorn, *Restoring Sexual Sanity: Christians in the Wake of the
Sexual Revolution* (Ft. Lauderdale, FL: Coral Ridge Ministries, 2000), p. 196.

any in mine." That is denial, not reality. All churches have sexual sinners.

(b) Delegation. The subject of sexual purity is not threatening to some pastors, but neither do they want to personally be involved in leading a purity ministry. They would rather delegate that responsibility to a staff pastor or motivated layperson.

(c) Determination. Some pastors respond with determination knowing that sexual sin and addiction is an issue in their congregations. They willingly and courageously lead their congregations into launching a sexual purity ministry.

Many pastors know that sexual immorality is an issue for their churches, but they have lacked the tools and education to know what to do. One of the reasons the National Coalition For Purity was created was to meet the needs for tools and education for pastors. However, if the church in general is to stand against the tsunami of sexual immorality flooding the culture, more than a handful of determined pastors will be needed. The church needs an army of determined pastors who will lead their churches into sexual purity.

Why This Book Was Written

This book is about sexual purity. While there are many types of purity—physical purity, emotional purity, spiritual purity, relational purity, religious purity, purity of motive, purity of speech, and purity of thinking, this book is intentionally focused on sexual purity. Why write a book on sexual purity? For four important reasons:

(a) Because God is holy. He is called the Holy One (Hosea 11:9). The words "holy" or "holiness" are used 651 times in the Bible. The doctrine of holiness is one of the most frequently described in the Bible. This is not unexpected, for holiness is God's primary attribute. It defines who He is. Holiness even takes precedence over love as God's primary attribute. God's love is based upon His holiness. It is because God is holy and must punish sin that His great love for us compelled Him to send His Son to the cross to die in our place. This book is dedicated to holding forth the holiness of God for all to see.

(b) Because we, as Christians, are called to be like God, to be holy (1 Pet. 1:15–16). We are to live holy, sexually-pure lives. After ministering to over 5,000 men through Every Man's Battle For Purity, it is more apparent than ever that God has a far higher standard of holiness than we have. His higher standard is that by which we must measure ourselves. That is why He can command it. This book is a clarion call to the church to obey the command of God to be holy, to call us to His higher standard of holiness.

(c) Because the church has been inundated and infiltrated by the sexualized culture surrounding her. We have been taught to "be in the world but not of the world." Unfortunately the church has become "of the world." The statistics on divorce, pornography consumption, teenage pregnancy, adultery, cohabitation, and sexually-transmitted diseases are not lying. The church has been impacted by the world. Perhaps in our effort to be culturally relevant we have lost sight of holiness. This book is a "finger-in-the-dike," attempting to hold back the raging waters of the culture.

(d) Finally, because the church is reticent to address the issue of sexual purity. Why? There could be many reasons. It could be because a large number of pastors are sexual sinners. It could be because many pastors are living pure lives and assume the same is true for their parishioners. It could be because pastors don't want to "rock the boat" by addressing such a volatile subject that many regard as unmentionable in polite society. For whatever reason, this book seeks to make sexual purity an unavoidable issue for the church and her pastors.

The Audience For This Book

This book was written for Christians. Believing that salvation must precede sanctification, this book was written for Christians because Christians are the ones called to be holy (1 Pet. 1:15–16). Only Christians possess the Holy Spirit (Rom. 8:9, 1 Cor. 6:19–20). Only Christians have the power through the indwelling Holy Spirit to be holy (1 Pet. 1:15, 2 Pet. 3:11). Non-Christians are called to be saved (Acts 13:47) and then sanctified (made holy).

CHAPTER TWO
THE GOD OF PURITY

Above him were seraphs ... And they were calling to one another: "Holy, holy, holy is the LORD Almighty; the whole earth is full of his glory."

Isaiah 6:2–3

The Priority of Purity to God

When it comes to sexual purity, much of the Bride of Christ is dressed in gray. In her position in Christ, the church is clothed in white garments, the righteousness of Christ, but in her practice, many believers have compromised with the world and the "passing pleasures of sin." This worldliness puts us on a collision course with God. Worldliness is sin (James 4:4). God is holy and must punish sin. His desire for the people made in His image is that they be holy even as He is holy (1 Pet. 1:16). As the apostle Paul writes, Christ's desire for the Bride is "to present her to himself as a radiant church, without stain or wrinkle or any other blemish, but holy and blameless" (Eph. 5:27). Purity is so important to God that He sent His Son to die on the cross. This chapter addresses the twin issues of the image of God and the holiness of God. Both doctrines define and empower a life of purity.

The Image of God

Giving Glory to God

The Westminster Shorter Catechism asks: "What is the chief end of man?" The answer: "Man's chief end is to glorify God and to enjoy Him forever."[10] Our purpose in life is to bring glory to our Creator. Theologians describe God's glory as being like blindingly bright light. Lewis and Demarest describe God's glory as, "... closely related to that of light. *Doxa* [glory] signifies the manifestation of God's incomparable brightness and splendor. It is the luminous display of God's very being and attributes."[11] The apostle Paul reinforces this idea when he declares, "[God] who alone is immortal and who lives in unapproachable light, whom no one has seen or can see ..." (1 Tim. 6:16). God is glorified when we become like Him, reflecting His character, doing His will. Jesus said, "This is to my Father's glory, that you bear much fruit, showing yourselves to be my disciples" (John 15:8). We exist to glorify God by reflecting His character and doing His will. As forgiven sinners, we are being transformed into Christ's glory (2 Cor. 3:18), the image of God.[12]

The Image and Likeness of God

No matter how tarnished humans are by sin, they are still made in the

---

[10]   Office of the General Assembly, *The Shorter Catechism. In The Constitution of the Presbyterian Church (U.S.A.): Part 1, Book of Confessions* (New York, NY: The Office of the General Assembly, 1983), p. 7.001-.010.
[11]   Gordon R. Lewis & Bruce A. Demarest, *Integrative Theology* (Vol. 2). Grand Rapids, MI: Zondervan Publishing House, 1996), p. 1:192.
[12]   "For Paul the restoration of the *imago* [image] means that the believer progressively becomes like Christ, who in a unique sense is the image [*eikōn*] of God ... The link between Christ and the renewed *imago* is that the Son, who shares God's very nature, is the head and prototype of the new humanity God is bringing into existence. The Christian's conformity to Christ is a process that begins in this life. So Paul affirms that "we, who with unveiled faces all reflect the Lord's glory, are being transformed into his likeness [*eikōn*] with ever-increasing glory" (2 Cor. 3:18; cf. Gal. 4:19), Ibid., p. 2:139, 140.

image and likeness of God. They are still God's highest creations. Humans are still image-bearers of the living God. What does it mean that men and women bear the "image and likeness" of God? This theological idea is the source of much controversy within Christendom. Is "image" the same as "likeness," or do they connote different things? Roman Catholic theology teaches that they are distinct and separate entities. However, Scripture does not support that they are technically distinct expressions, but rather that they connote the same thing. All people, regardless of race, gender, nationality, or ethnicity, bear the image of God. It is what distinguishes humans from animals. Because all humans possess the image of God, murder is forbidden and is a violation of God's commandments (Exod. 20:13). Although humans bear the image of God, Jesus Christ is the ultimate image-bearer (2 Cor. 4:4; Col. 1:15). Jesus is the visible presence of God in human form. Through the process of the new birth and transformed life, believers are being shaped into the likeness of Christ, the perfect image of God.[13]

Following the fall of man into sin, the retained image of God means that humans possess some but not all of God's attributes. Attributes which humans do not possess include self-existence, immutability, or omnipotence, but, like God, they do have personality. They have volitional freedom, intelligence, rationality, and creativity. All these are qualities first found in God yet retained in humans despite the fall. Humans are moral beings endowed with a conscience to know right and wrong. Like God, they have the capacity for holiness, love, justice, mercy, and truth. Finally, like God, humans are capable of dominion. As God rules all creation, humans have the right and

---

[13] James R. Beck & Bruce Demarest, *The Human Person in Theology and Psychology* (Grand Rapids, MI: Kregel Publications, 2005), pp. 150-153.

responsibility to rule the earth (cf. Gen. 1:26).[14] Providing good insight on the nature of the image of God, Longman says:

> The term "image" is used in describing a king who sets up images of himself all across his kingdom to remind people who is king. When we look at each other we are reminded of our God because we reflect some of his attributes. The fact that we are created in the image of God gives us the basis for anthropomorphic terms for God. The reason why we are commanded not to make an image of God is that we are the only divinely-authorized images of God.[15]

How did the fall affect the image of God in humans?

When humankind fell through sin, what of the image and likeness of God was defiled? When humans sinned and fell, what of the divine image and likeness of God was lost and what was retained? Rom. 3:23 declares, "For all have sinned and fall short of the glory of God…" When Adam and Eve sinned and fell in the garden, they lost some of the glorious image of God they once possessed. But what of that image has been retained? The Bible declares that Adam and Eve, though created in the image and likeness of God and designed for relationship with God, fell from that relationship through sin (Gen. 2–3). Now, as Anthony Hoekema writes, "Fallen man is still an image-bearer of God … but that image has apparently been so corrupted or spoiled through man's fall into sin that he needs once again to be conformed to that image."[16]

---

[14] E. McChesney in Merrill F. Unger, *Unger's Bible Dictionary* (Chicago, IL: Moody Press, 1977), p. 517.

[15] Tremper I. Longman, *Biblical Exegesis and Marriage and Family Class Notes* (Paper presented at Denver Seminary, Denver, CO, July 28-30, 2004).

[16] Anthony A. Hoekema, *Created in God's Image* (Grand Rapids, MI: William B. Eerdmans Publishing Company, 1994), pp. 17, 23.

Man's fall into sin caused holistic depravity.

To what degree has man been corrupted by the fall? Adam and Eve's sin caused holistic depravity, meaning that sin affected every part of man—body, soul, and spirit. Infants are born with an inherited sin nature from Adam and are born affected by sin in every part of their beings. Holistic depravity does not mean that mankind is as bad as they possibly could be. It simply means that they have been impacted in all parts of their being by sin. Yet despite being corrupted by sin in their total beings, humans still bear the image and likeness of God. Humans still retain much of the image of God they once possessed before they fell into sin. Like God, humans are spiritual in nature and immortal. Men and women will never die, for they will spend eternity either in heaven or in the lake of fire. Yet on a spiritual level, they are fallen and in order to become conformed to the image of God, they must be "born again" (John 3:3).

Jesus is the image of God.

In the Bible, Jesus Christ is called the "image of the invisible God" (Col. 1:15) and "the exact representation of his [God's] being" (Heb. 1:3). Jesus is the ultimate image of God. As McChesney notes, "In the Old Testament man appears created after the image of God; in the New, the Son is the prototype of redeemed or renewed humanity."[17] Erickson encourages us to be like Christ by declaring:

> We should pattern ourselves after Jesus, who is the complete
> revelation of what the image of God is. He is the full image of
> God, and he is the one person whose humanity was never spoiled
> by sinning (Heb. 4:15). If we wish to know the outworking of

---

[17]   McChesney in *Unger's Bible Dictionary*, p. 517.

the image of God, we can see it in Jesus.[18]

Renewing the image of God.

The *sanctification* process is God's work of renewing the image of God in sinners. *Glorification* is the process completed and the image of God restored. Recovery of the image of God is the underlying theological foundation for any purity ministry. The reason we are called to become sexually pure is that God is holy and we bear His image and likeness.

How is the image of God renewed in humans? It is through the power of Christ as mediated through the indwelling Holy Spirit. Lewis and Demarest state, "Christ died to restore the divine image, renewing our abilities to know, love, and serve the transcendent God in creation."[19] The role of the Holy Spirit is to progressively conform us to the image of Christ (Rom. 8:29). The Spirit renews the minds of believers, giving them the capacity to understand, think, and reason morally. The ultimate expression of this renewal is found in the age to come when our minds will be completely renewed without the taint of sin (1 Cor. 13:12). Through the sanctifying power of the Holy Spirit, believers "are being transformed into his likeness with ever-increasing glory, which comes from the Lord, who is the Spirit" (2 Cor. 3:18).

The progressive renewing of the image of God by the Holy Spirit in the believer impacts every facet of the believer's life—mind, will, emotions, mood, creativity, conscience, relationships, work, and play. All are subject to the Spirit's transforming power as He shapes believers into the very image of Jesus Christ. Now regenerated humans are capable of communicating and connecting with God, self, and others. "The image will thus emerge as

---

[18] Millard J. Erickson, *Christian Theology* (Grand Rapids, MI: Baker Book House, 1988), p. 515.

[19] Lewis & Demarest, *Integrative Theology,* p. 2:404.

a rich, multi-faceted reality, comprising acts, relations, capacities, virtues, dispositions, and even emotions."[20] "The *imago Dei* [image of God], impaired and enslaved by the fall, is rejuvenated" by the Spirit's work of regeneration.[21]

The Holiness of God

God is holy (1 Pet. 1:18–19) and love (1 John 4:16). So must we be. Both God's holiness and love inform His judgment. His holiness demands justice and punishment for sinners in the judgment. His love pleads for mercy and forgiveness for sinners in the judgment. Both God's holiness and love meet at

> "Both God's holiness and love meet at the cross of Jesus Christ."

the cross of Jesus Christ. On the cross Christ met God's standards of the law (Matt. 5:17). On the cross Christ became sin so that sinners who believe in Him might be declared righteous (2 Cor. 5:21). Jesus is God, holy and loving, just and merciful. Sinners who accept Him by faith receive redemption and forgiveness of their sins (Eph. 1:7).

Definitions of Holiness

A key concept under the category of the image and likeness of God is the holiness of God. God is holy, and he calls His people to be holy (1 Pet. 1:15–16). What does it mean that God is holy? The Hebrew word translated *holy*, carries the idea of "separation or withdrawal."[22] Erickson states that it

---

[20] Alvin Plantinga, "Images of God," in *Christian Faith and Practice in the Modern Practice in the Modern World* (Grand Rapids, MI: William B. Eerdmans Publishing Company, 1988), p. 52.

[21] Lewis & Demarest, *Integrative Theology,* p. 3:105.

[22] קָדוֹשׁ [qadosh] "holy", Francis Brown, S. R. Driver, & Charles A. Briggs, *A Hebrew and English Lexicon of the Old Testament* (Oxford, England: The Clarendon Press, 1972), p. 871.

means, "marked off" or "withdrawn from common, ordinary use."[23] It captures

the qualities of being unique, special, separate from sin and sinners. Sproul

declares, "The things that are holy are things that are set apart, separated from

the rest. They have been consecrated, separated from the commonplace, unto

the Lord and to his service."[24] In describing the Lord's reign on the earth,

Zech. 14:20–21 says that even the bells of horses and every cooking pot in the

land of Judah will be inscribed with "holy to the Lord."[25] Everything will be

set apart as holy and dedicated to the Lord.

The New Testament word for *holy* means, "dedicated to God, holy,

sacred, i.e., reserved for God and his service."[26] When applied to people, it

means, "to consecrate, dedicate, sanctify, i.e., include in the inner circle of

what is holy, in both religious and moral uses of the word."[27] The Hebrew

word focuses on the separateness of holiness. The Greek word draws our

attention to the dedication of the object or person to God and His service.

Combined, we begin to grasp the power of holiness. Holy people are people

set apart for God's use. Holy people separate themselves from the common

and the unclean. Holy people are special to God and under the anointing of

His Holy Spirit.

God is holy and separate from sin and sinners. He is separate from

the earth and all that is finite. God is morally perfect. He is so holy, so pure,

that nothing unclean or defiled can enter His presence. Concerning God's

holiness, Lewis and Demarest declare, "Because God is infinitely holy and

---

[23] Erickson, *Christian Theology*, p. 284.

[24] R. C. Sproul, *The Holiness of God*. (Wheaton, IL: Tyndale House Publishers, Inc., 1985), p. 56.

[25] קֹדֶשׁ לַיהוָה [*qedesh la Yahweh*] "holy to the Lord"

[26] Arndt & Gingrich, p. 9.

[27] Ibid., p. 8.

righteous He can have no fellowship with unrighteousness in any form. Consequently those who constitute God's new society [the church] must themselves be holy."[28]

The Command to be Holy

God's holiness shows itself in numerous purity texts in the Bible including: "You shall not commit adultery" (Exod. 20:14), "Flee from sexual immorality. All other sins a man commits are outside his body, but he who sins sexually sins against his own body" (1 Cor. 6:18), and "Since we have these promises, dear friends, let us purify ourselves from everything that contaminates body and spirit, perfecting holiness out of reverence for God" (2 Cor. 7:1). Holiness is the primary attribute of God from which all others flow. He is first and foremost holy. No unclean thing can come into His presence (Isa. 52:11, 2 Cor. 6:17). He commands His sons and daughters to be holy even as He is (1 Pet. 1:16). Only the holy have access to the Holy One of Israel.

The standard of holiness.

The standard of holiness is God not us. We are too lenient with ourselves and give ourselves permission to sin. We measure holiness against others and declare ourselves "holier than thou." Our standards shift with our moods and the company we keep. We declare ourselves, "good enough" even in the face of our hypocrisy. As Jeremiah, the prophet, declared, "The heart is deceitful above all things and beyond cure. Who can understand it?" (Jer. 17:9).

"When one measures one's holiness, not against the standard of oneself or of other humans, but against God, the need for a complete change

---

[28] Lewis & Demarest, *Integrative Theology,* p. 3:173.

of moral and spiritual condition becomes apparent," writes Erickson.[29] Strong

tells us, "According to the Scriptures, the ground of moral obligation is the

holiness of God."[30]

Is holiness the same as purity?

Is holiness the same as purity? No, it is not. Holiness is a broader

term that encompasses purity. Purity is one aspect of holiness. R. C. Sproul

helps us understand the difference:

> Where does purity come in? We are so accustomed to equating
>
> holiness with purity or ethical perfection that we look for the idea
>
> when the word *holy* appears. When things are made holy, when they
>
> are consecrated, they are set apart unto purity. They are to be used
>
> in a pure way. They are to reflect purity as well as simple apartness.
>
> Purity is not excluded from the idea of the holy; it is contained within
>
> it. But the point we must remember is that the idea of the holy is
>
> never exhausted by the idea of purity. It includes purity but is much
>
> more than that. It is purity and transcendence. It is a transcendent
>
> purity.[31]

How do we become holy?

How do we become holy even as God is holy? "God alone is holy in

himself. Only God can sanctify something else. Only God can put the touch

on something that changes it from the commonplace to something special,

different, and apart."[32] If Christians are going to become holy like God, it will

not be because they have achieved this state in the flesh. Only God can make

---

[29]   Erickson, p. 286.

[30]   Augustus H. Strong, *Systematic Theology* (Valley Forge, PA.: Judson Press, 1972), p. 302.

[31]   Sproul, p. 57.

[32]   Ibid., p. 56.

us holy. Is abstaining from sexual sin enough? Storms shares his insights on how we become holy when he declares, "The key to holiness is, once again, falling in love with Jesus."[33] Storms elaborates:

> Volitional restraint and abstinence are only effective against sin when the soul embraces a pleasure superior to the one denied. There is little sanctifying value in depriving our souls of fleshly entertainment if steps are not taken to feast on all that God is for us in Jesus ... Finding fullness of joy and everlasting pleasure in God's presence alone will serve to woo our wayward hearts from the power of the world, the flesh, and the devil. Therefore, falling in love with the Son of God is the key to holiness.[34]

Holiness and sanctification.

Sanctification is the doctrine of being "set apart for God" or made holy. It has past, present, and future aspects to it in much the same way that salvation does. In Christ Jesus we have been made holy and perfect (1 Cor. 6:11). That is our positional sanctification and it is the past aspect of sanctification. In our present state, we are being made holy through trials and suffering (2 Pet. 3:11). That is the present aspect of sanctification. It is our practice of sanctification. When Jesus returns to call us to Himself, we shall be made holy and perfect (1 John 3:2). That is the future sanctification of believers.[35]

The apostle Paul clearly articulates the need for practical sanctification when he wrote to the Corinthian church saying, "Since we have these promises, dear friends, let us purify ourselves from everything that

---

[33] Storms, p. 81.

[34] Ibid., pp. 103, 104.

[35] Neil T. Anderson & Robert L. Saucy, *The Common Made Holy* (Eugene, OR: Harvest House Publishers, 1997), pp. 39-55.

contaminates body and spirit, perfecting holiness out of reverence for God" (2 Cor. 7:1). The church in Corinth was already sanctified in their position in Christ Jesus (1 Cor. 1:2), yet Paul reminded them of their calling to be holy in their practice.

How do we become more pure?

Because purity is the practical application of holiness, a purity ministry will teach men, women, and teens how to flee sexual immorality (1 Cor. 6:18), discipline themselves by guarding their eyes, take captive immoral thoughts, praying, and reading the Word daily (cf. Heb. 12: 11, 2 Cor. 10:5), hold one another accountable to live in purity (cf. Heb. 4:13), restore their marriages (1 Cor. 7:10–11), and practice self-control (1 Cor. 7:8–9). Holiness must move from being a doctrine that is intellectually embraced by believers to a lifestyle that characterizes every aspect of their beings. Holiness must be made practical for the Bride of Christ.

Making holiness practical

Why launch a purity ministry in a local church? To be holy even as God is holy. The Bible tells us that in our position in Christ we are holy, but in our practice we need to become holy. A purity ministry is concerned with present sanctification, equipping the people of God to live holy lives. It makes holiness practical for God's people. It gives pastors the tools they need and the practical strategy for using those tools so they can purify the flock God has entrusted to them. It is a "boot-on-the-ground" ministry making holiness practical for men, women, and teens.

CHAPTER THREE
GOD'S DESIGN FOR SEXUALITY

Marriage should be honored by all, and the marriage bed kept pure, for God will judge the adulterer and all the sexually immoral.

Hebrews 13:4

God's Purpose and Design for Human Sexuality

God Created Sex and Called it Very Good

On the sixth day of creation, God created man in His own image, male and female He created them and told them to be fruitful and multiply and fill the earth (Gen. 1:27, 28). What we call a "sex drive" is essentially the command of God "to be fruitful and multiply" written on the heart of every man and woman. God never issues a command without providing the resources to obey it. Sexual reproduction was God's creation. It was His resource for obeying the command to be "fruitful and multiply and fill the earth." After creating man, the Bible says, "God saw all that he had made [including sexual reproduction], and it was very good ..." (Gen. 1:31). Sex was part of the basic nature of humans—defining who they were as male and female and differentiating them from one another and the rest of creation (cf. Gen. 2:20). Sex was part of God's blessing pronounced upon man (Gen. 1:28). Sex was created before the fall of man into sin and was without any taint of sin. Hoekema writes of Genesis 1:26, "The injunction to be fruitful and multiply implies the institution of marriage, the establishment of which is narrated in the second chapter of Genesis (vv. 18–24)."[36] Hoekema goes on to note, "In giving his blessing, God promises to enable human beings to propagate and bring forth children who will fill the earth."[37] Sex was God's enablement. Anderson and Mylander (2006) write:

> Adam was drawn to Eve the moment he saw her. They saw each other as male and female, yet one flesh. They recognized both their differences and their oneness. God used their masculinity and femininity to both differentiate them and unite them. They were naked and unashamed. Sexual attraction and passion were present before the fall. Sex was not evil; it was God's plan. The fall only perverted what God had created to be good.[38]

God's Many Purposes for Human Sexuality

Sex was meant to bond husbands and wives in marriage.

Besides reproduction of the human race, God designed sex for a number of reasons. God tells us that "every good and perfect gift is from above, coming down from the Father ..." (James 1:17). Sex, as God intended it, is His good and perfect gift to humanity. Besides procreation, God designed sex to unite husbands and wives in marriage causing them to become "one flesh" (Gen. 2:24). As a side note, it is interesting that marriage ("leaving") precedes intercourse ("cleaving" NASV) in God's design. The Hebrew word

---

[36] Hoekema, p. 14.

[37] Ibid., p. 14.

[38] Neil T. Anderson & Charles Mylander, *Experiencing Christ Together* (Eugene, OR: Harvest House Publishers, 2006), p. 25.

in Genesis 2:24 captures the idea of sexual union of husband and wife.[39] The bonding power of sex is described by Paul in 1 Corinthians 6:16, "Do you not know that he who unites himself with a prostitute is one with her in body? For it is said, 'The two will become one flesh.' "

Sex was meant to be pleasurable.

Additionally, sex was created by God to be pleasurable for husbands and wives. God could have made human reproduction devoid of pleasure, but He didn't. This counters the traditional Roman Catholic view that intercourse is for procreation only. Anderson comments on the pleasure aspect of sex when he writes:

Intimate sexual relationships were not separate from their [Adam and Eve] relationship with God. There was no sin and nothing to hide, so Adam and Eve had no reason to cover up their nakedness ... Sex was intended for procreation as well as pleasure. They didn't "make" love. Sexual intercourse and physical touch were means by which the two could express their love to each other and multiply. They were afforded a tremendous amount of freedom as long as they remained in a dependent relationship with God.[40]

Probably no other book in the Bible illustrates the pleasure of human sexuality better than Song of Songs. A collection of love poems, Song of Songs is included in the Bible to show us how God feels about sex. Song of Songs should be taken literally, not as an allegory of Christ's love for the church. As Longman states:

---

[39] דָּבַק [*dabaq*] "cleave," Longman, *Biblical Exegesis*, p. 3.
[40] Neil T. Anderson, *Winning the Battle Within* (Eugene, OR: Harvest House Publishers, 2008), p. 16.

The presence of Song of Songs opens the door for Christians to realize that God has given his people marital sex for their enjoyment ... Most of the rest of Scripture draws boundaries around sexuality to speak about its prohibitions. Song of Songs takes a positive look at biblical, marital sexuality. God is interested in us as whole people—body, soul, and spirit. God loves us as whole people including our sexuality.[41]

As an example of the pleasure God intended sex to be for couples, consider Song of Songs 5. This love poem is filled with double entendre and sexual euphemism. As Longman notes:

... part of that double entendre is that he [the husband] is asking her to open up to him sexually. After all, the door, unmentioned but implied in his request, is a long-standing symbol for entry into a woman's body ... The door is clearly a euphemism for a woman's vagina, and an open door denotes a sexually available woman.[42]

Sex was meant to be the ultimate expression of intimacy.

Longman comments on Genesis 2:25, "It is precisely in the area of sexuality ('nakedness') that their intimacy and total vulnerability to one another is expressed most powerfully. In the Garden, Adam and Eve experienced harmony and complete vulnerability toward one another."[43] Before the fall, Adam and Eve had perfect intimacy with God and one another. Genesis 2:25 indicates that the first couple experienced an innocence about their nakedness. Shame was not connected to nakedness because sin

---

[41] Longman, *Biblical Exegesis*, p. 1.
[42] Tremper I. Longman, *Song of Songs*, (Grand Rapids, MI: William B. Eerdmans Publishing Company, 2001), p. 166.
[43] Ibid., p. 64.

had not perverted their sexuality. Sexual union flowed naturally out of that kind of relational intimacy. It is not without justification that dispensational theologians call this period of time the "dispensation of innocence."[44]

The Fall Perverted Human Sexuality

God created sex pre-fall and called it very good. Sex was an integral component in uniting Adam and Eve, causing them to become one flesh. One of the most immediate results of disobeying God in Genesis 3 was the realization by Adam and Eve that they were naked (Gen. 3:7). With that realization, the first couple sewed fig leaves together to form coverings for themselves. The King James Version of the Bible calls them "aprons." Schaeffer comments on the term:

> The word *aprons* in the Hebrew is interesting. Actually, it simply means to "gird yourself about," so people have translated the word in various ways. One Bible, the Breeches Bible of 1608, got its name from the way it translated this word. But whatever an *apron* is, it is something one puts around himself.[45]

Why Adam and Eve covered themselves.

Why did Adam and Eve cover their nakedness after the fall? Because their intimacy had been broken, and they knew it. Sin separates. It separates us from God and from one another. When the first pair sinned, they immediately harvested the bitter fruit of separation from one another. Their nakedness was now a source of shame. No longer did they feel free to be naked in one another's presence. "From vulnerability and openness they move to self-consciousness, which is seen in their concern with their nakedness. They now

---

[44] Cyrus I . Scofield, *The Scofield Reference Bible* (New York, NY: Oxford University, 1945), p. 5.

[45] Francis Schaeffer, *Genesis in Space and Time: The Flow of Biblical History* (Downers Grove, IL: InterVarsity Press, 1972), p. 91.

have something to hide."[46]

A second reason why they wrapped something around themselves is pointed out by Stanley et al., "... the couple no longer felt the glorious freedom of utter acceptance, so *they covered up where they were most obviously different.*"[47] For the first time, Adam and Eve experienced fear—fear of punishment and fear of rejection.

The spread of sexual perversion.

Besides the fear, shame, and loss of intimacy caused by Adam and Eve's disobedience, the fall incurred God's curse and with it death became the common lot of humanity. The fall from innocence also perverted human sexuality. No longer was sex solely the expression of innocence and the fruit of intimacy and love. Soon after the fall sexual relationships became perverted as the murderous Lamech married two women (Gen. 4:19) in clear disobedience of God's monogamous design for marriage. Then sex jumped the boundaries of heterosexuality to homosexuality as the men of Sodom and Gomorrah attempted to rape the two angelic messengers sent by God to warn Lot (Gen. 19:4). Before the Genesis account is finished, it records the first instance of incestuous sex as the two daughters of Lot shamelessly had intercourse with their drunken father (Gen. 19:30–37). There follows the rape of Dinah, daughter of Jacob and Leah, by Shechem (Gen. 34:2), and the seduction of Judah by his daughter-in-law, Tamar (Gen. 38:18). All these examples show sex being used as a weapon to achieve selfish purposes. Whether used for lust, manipulation, or retribution, sex has moved far from the innocence of Eden. No longer is it confined solely to a loving,

---

[46] Longman, *Song of Songs*, p. 65.

[47] Scott Stanley, et al., *A Lasting Promise: A Christian Guide to Fighting for Your Marriage* (San Francisco, CA: Jossey-Bass Publishers, 1998), p. 20.

heterosexual, monogamous marriage. Sin has perverted the good gift of God.
Sex has clearly moved outside the protective boundaries of God's original
design and purpose.

The Dangers of Sexual Immorality

So God's original purpose and design for human sexuality was
quickly perverted after the fall of man into sin. The sin of sexual immorality
was woven into the fabric of the human race. What constitutes sexual
immorality and why is it a danger to God's design for human sexuality and
marriage? Is there a connection between sexual immorality and the heart, or is
sexual immorality simply a physical act?

The Characteristics of Sexual Immorality

Definitions of sexual immorality.

What is sexual immorality? In Hebrew the primary verb for sexual
immorality is often translated as "fornication or whoredom" in the King James
Version of the Bible.[48] Brown, Driver, and Briggs say it means to "commit
fornication, be a harlot."[49] It's significant that the term is often used to
describe Israel's idolatry of spurning the Lord God to "prostitute themselves"
to other deities (cf. Exod. 34:15–16; Lev. 17:7, 20:5; Deut. 31:16; Judg. 2:17,
8:27, 33). There is an immorality-idolatry connection that we will explore
later. It should be noted that the same Hebrew verb with slightly different
vowel pointing means to "reject or spurn" and is used of God rejecting His
people (Ps. 43:2; 60:3; 77:7; 88:14; Zech. 10:6).[50] The pattern of Israel is
predictable: sexual immorality leads to idolatry which leads to rejection by
God. Israel is God's wife, and for her to run after other deities is nothing less

---

[48] הָנָז [*zanah*] "fornication, whoredom"
[49] Brown, Driver, Briggs, *A Hebrew and English Lexicon*, p. 275.
[50] הָנָז, [*zanah*] "reject, spurn," Ibid., p. 276.

than spiritual adultery. God will not tolerate unfaithfulness from His wife, so He releases her into the discipline of other nations.

The primary New Testament noun for sexual immorality is πορνεία [*porneia*], which Arndt and Gingrich understand to mean, "prostitution, unchastity, fornication, of every kind of unlawful sexual intercourse."[51] Sexual immorality is typically distinguished in the New Testament from the Greek word for adultery[52] (Matt. 15:19; 1 Cor. 6:9; Heb. 13:4). Sexual immorality is a larger term than adultery. Although occasionally translated as "adultery" or "fornication," πορνεία is an "umbrella" term encompassing any "unlawful sexual intercourse." The Greek word μοιχεία [*moichea*] is always translated "adultery" in the New Testament.

The noun, *porneia,* is used to render Jesus' words in Matthew 5:32, 15:19, 19:9; Mark 7:21; and John 8:41. The NIV translates *porneia* as "adultery" (Matt. 5:32), "sexual immorality" (Matt. 15:19), "marital unfaithfulness" and "adultery" (Matt. 19:9), "sexual immorality" (Mark 7:21), and "illegitimate" (John 8:41).

What constitutes sexual immorality?

If *porneia* constitutes "unlawful sexual intercourse," what would Jesus have understood unlawful sexual intercourse to be? I believe He would have understood it to mean the sexual immorality specified under the law. In Leviticus. 18:1–23, the Lord God, through Moses, told the children of Israel that He forbids the unlawful sexual practices of the nations. He told Israel they must not follow their practices but rather listen to the Lord their God and live as a clean and distinctly different people. Although the King James

---

[51] Arndt and Gingrich, p. 699. Every time I use the English term, "sexual immorality" it is a translation of the Greek word πορνεία [*porneia*]

[52] Μοιχεία [*moicheia*] "adultery"

Version refers to the sins catalogued in Leviticus 18:1–18 as "uncovering the nakedness" of another, Keil and Delitsch and others understand the phrase to be a euphemism for "sexual intercourse."[53] The Lord lists the following unlawful sexual practices His people were to avoid: (a) incest with any close relative including sexual intercourse with one's mother (18:7), stepmother (18:8), sister (18:9), stepsister (18:9), daughter (18:10), daughter-in-law (18:10, 15), niece (18:10), sister-in-law (18:11, 16), aunt (18:12–14), a woman and her daughter or daughter-in-law (18:17); (b) polygamy (18:18); (c) menstrual sex (18:19); (d) adultery (18:20); (e) idolatry (which must have included a form of sexual sin) (18:21); (f) homosexuality (18:22); and (g) bestiality (18:23). In addition to the sexual sins listed in Leviticus 18, the sins of transvestism (Deut. 22:5), fornication (Deut. 22:20–24), and rape (Deut. 22:25–27) are also condemned as unlawful.

Furthermore, Jesus understood adultery as more than a physical act. He understood it to include emotional infidelity. In Matthew 5:27–28, Jesus redressed the distortion of the law regarding adultery. He declared, "You have heard that it was said, 'Do not commit adultery.' But I tell you that anyone who looks at a woman lustfully has already committed adultery with her in his heart." Jesus told us that God's definition of what constitutes adultery goes beyond the external physical act. It goes to the internal attitude of the heart. The adulterous heart betrays its nature through lustful looks and emotional infidelity. An emotional attachment to someone other than one's spouse is emotional adultery and is regarded by God as the same as physical sexual adultery.

---

[53] C. F. Keil, & Franz Delitzsch, *The Pentateuch*. In C. F. Keil, & F. Delitzsch, *Commentary on the Old Testament* (J. Martin, Trans., Vol. 1). Grand Rapids, MI: William B. Eerdmans Publishing Company, (n.d.). p. 412.

The dangers of sexual immorality.

Why are all these sexually immoral practices dangerous? In the case of rape or incest they are violations of one's personal freedom of choice, and all are violations of God's pattern for sexual expression within marriage. However, their primary danger lies in being entry points into idolatry. Sexual sins break down the moral standards of God and seduce the hearts of God's people into idolatry, worshiping the creature rather than the Creator. The apostle Paul described this connection in Romans 1:21–32 when he explained humanity's descent into depravity. Paul wrote that the descent begins when men and women become arrogant and foolish and think themselves wiser than God. They soon desert the knowledge of the living God (1:21–22). Thinking they know better than God, they trade the worship of God for idolatry (1:23). Worshiping idols (the creature) invariably leads to sexual idolatry (1:24–25). Sexual idolatry is expressed through all manner of sexual immorality including homosexuality (1:26–27). The descent culminates with some of the most frightening words used in the Bible, God "gave them over to a depraved mind" (1:28) which leads to a plethora of sins.

Sexual Immorality Is a Heart Issue

All sexual activity, godly or ungodly, begins in the heart. We are to love God and one another from the heart (Matt. 22:37; 1 Pet. 1:22). The Bible tells us that the heart is more than a physical organ. It is the center of our being where our values are stored, where thinking takes place, and where decisions are made. Jesus said, "For out of the heart come evil thoughts, murder, adultery, sexual immorality, theft, false testimony, slander" (Matt. 15:19). All actions begin in the heart.

The real issue behind all sexual immorality is a rebel heart that seeks to meet needs independently of God. Schaumburg recognizes this fact. He writes:

> The origin of what is today called sexual addiction lies in the human heart's stubborn determination to obtain what only God in His grace can provide. It is foolish to exhort sex addicts to stop their behavior. Addicts become powerless over their behavior not because it's a disease but because God has responded to the arrogance of the human heart by turning people over to the control of their evil desires.[54]

Flee Sexual Immorality

The Bible sounds a clear warning regarding sexual immorality. "Flee from sexual immorality ..." shouts the apostle in 1 Corinthians 6:18. We are not told to fight immorality but to flee it. In fact, as a present imperative, the Greek verb for "flee" means "continually flee" sexual immorality.[55] Like Joseph when he was confronted with the adulterous proposition of Potiphar's wife (Gen. 39:12), we are to run for our lives! Why should we flee sexual immorality? The apostle Paul gives us multiple reasons in 1 Corinthians 6:12–20:

(a) Mastery. It can master us (6:12)

(b) Glorification. As Christians our bodies are to be used to glorify God (6:13)

(c) Resurrection. Our bodies will be resurrected someday (6:14)

(d) Union. Our bodies are members of Christ (6:15)

(e) Bonding. Sexual immorality is physically and emotionally

---

[54] Schaumburg, p. 73.

[55] Φεύγετε [pheugete] "flee"

bonding. It causes us to form a one-flesh union with another person (6:16)

(f) Unique. Sexual immorality is a unique sin in that it is a sin against one's own body (6:18)

(g) Spiritual. Our bodies are the temple of the Holy Spirit, his dwelling place (6:19)

(h) Legal. We don't own our bodies, but rather Christ does. He bought them with his blood (6:19–20). In fact, according to Paul, spouses "own" each other's bodies (1 Cor. 7:4).

Sexual Immorality Is a Unique Sin

What does the apostle Paul mean when he says, "All other sins a man commits are outside his body, but he who sins sexually sins against his own body" (1 Cor. 6:18)? In what way is sexual immorality a sin against one's own body? Suggested meanings for this difficult passage include:

(a) sexual immorality is a sin against one's personality[56]

(b) sexual immorality breaks the "mystical bond" between the body and Christ[57]

(c) sexual immorality is unique in that it afflicts the body with sexually transmitted diseases[58]

(d) sexual immorality touches "the springs of being," the heart[59]

(e) sexual immorality is a sin "wrought *within* the body," a denial of

---

[56] C. F. Moule, *An Idiom-Book of New Testament Greek* (London: Syndics of the Cambridge University Press, 1968), p. 197; Warren Wiersbe, *The Bible Exposition Commentary* (Wheaton, IL: Victor Books, 1989), p. 589.
[57] Archibald Thomas Robertson, *The Epistles of Paul* (Vol. 4) (Nashville, TN: Broadman Press, 1931), p. 122.
[58] Ibid., p. 123.
[59] G. G. Findlay, *St. Paul's First Epistle to the Corinthians*, in W. R. Nicoll (Ed.), *The Expositor's Greek Testament* (Vol. 2) (Grand Rapids, MI: William B. Eerdmans Publishing Company, 1970), p. 821.

union with Christ[60]

(f) sexual immorality "takes that body which is 'a member of Christ' and puts it into a union which 'blasts his own body'."[61]

To understand what makes sexual immorality unique, we must understand why all other sins are "outside" the body and why sexual sins are "against" the sinner's own body.[62] All sins affect us. Second Corinthians 7:1 exhorts Christians to purify themselves of "everything that contaminates body and spirit." Sins such as lying, stealing, bitterness, rage, anger, and unwholesome talk have both an external impact, in that they affect others, and an internal impact in grieving the Holy Spirit (Eph. 4:25–32) and defiling our souls. Sexual immorality, aside from the physical aspect of being a sin outside of one's body involving others and abusing one's own body (prostitutes, masturbation, adultery, incest, etc.), is also an internal sin. It is a unique sin in that it is different from every other sin—not worse, but different. Moule finds this notion disturbing. In commenting on 1 Corinthians 6:18 he writes:

> If it is *not* [a counterattack by St. Paul against an antinomian slogan of the libertines], then we are faced with the perplexity that St. Paul pronounces fornication to be *essentially* different (and not merely different in *degree)* from any other sort of sin—a position with which few modern Christians would

---

[60]   S. L. Johnson, *The First Epistle to the Corinthians*, in C. F. Pfeiffer & E. F. Harrison (Eds.), *The Wycliffe Bible Commentary* (Chicago, IL: Moody Press, 1972), p. 606.

[61]   Leon Morris, *The First Epistle of Paul to the Corinthians*, in R. V. Tasker (Ed.), *Tyndale New Testament Commentaries* (Vol. 7) (Grand Rapids, MI: William B. Eerdmans Publishing, 1975), p 102.

[62]   Paul uses the Greek phrase εἰς τὸ ἴδιον σῶμα [*eis to idion soma*], which literally means "against (εἰς used in a hostile sense) the own body," to contrast with ἐκτὸς τοῦ σώματός [*ektos tou somatos*], "outside the body."

agree.[63]

Sexual immorality, however, *is* a different sin. It is an attack against the spiritual oneness of the believer with Christ. The context (6:16–17, 19–20) informs us that at salvation the spirit of the believer is united to the Holy Spirit and is now in union (one) with Him. Furthermore, the body of the believer is now the very temple of the Holy Spirit. He dwells in it. Christ bought it for the Spirit with his blood and, as the owner, the body is Christ's possession to do with as He pleases. Sexual immorality threatens our oneness with Christ by committing spiritual adultery just as physical adultery threatens our marital union with our spouse.

> **"Sexual immorality, however, *is* a different sin."**

Many theologians favor a bipartite view of man, meaning that man is composed of two parts, material (body) and immaterial (soul-spirit). However, the Bible lends equal credence to humans being tripartite, meaning that people have three unique and identifiable parts: body, soul, and spirit. Each one is the person. Humans are designed and fashioned after the trinitarian God who made them. Sexual immorality, like all sin, affects all three parts of people— for all three parts of people are inextricably and inseparably woven together. Sexual immorality is unique in that it affects all three parts differently. Sexual immorality steals what belongs to Christ (the physical body) and uses it in a sinful act. Sexual immorality grieves the Holy Spirit (who dwells within) by doing that which is unholy. Sexual immorality wounds the soul by generating emotions such as fear, guilt, and shame, and by distorting the sinner's thinking.

---

[63] Moule, p. 196.

Finally, sexual immorality is a unique sin in a number of ways:

(a) Physically. Unlike any other sin, only sexual immorality can produce a soul that lives forever. A baby can be conceived through sexual immorality and the soul of that baby will spend eternity either in heaven or hell. Also, only sexual immorality can infect another with a sexually transmitted disease.

(b) Spiritually. Only sexual immorality attacks our union with Christ.

(c) Spiritually. Only sexual immorality can bind us to another person.

The Connection Between Sexual Immorality and Idolatry

Sexual Addiction Is Idolatry

Although the Bible never uses the term "addiction," it does use related terms such as "mastery," "slavery," and "bondage." Consider the words of Paul to the Corinthian church, " 'Everything is permissible for me'— but not everything is beneficial. 'Everything is permissible for me'— but I will not be mastered by anything" (1 Cor. 6:12). What does Paul mean when he quotes, "everything is permissible for me?" Does he mean that even sexual immorality is permissible for the believer? The phrase, "everything is permissible," is used four times by the apostle Paul (twice in 1 Cor. 6:12 and twice in 1 Cor. 10:23). In 1 Corinthians 6:12, the apostle personalizes the permission by declaring "for me."[64] The phrase, "everything is permissible," was a popular quote of some in Corinth and may have been quoted in the letter sent by the Corinthians to Paul.[65] Wiersbe writes, "This was a popular phrase in Corinth, based on a false view of Christian freedom. We have not been set free so that we can enter into a new kind of bondage!" [66] The apostle

---

[64] Greek word μοι [*moi*] "for me"
[65] Findlay, p. 818.
[66] Wiersbe, p. 588.

Paul uses the phrase as a contrast to the self-control and selfless living that should characterize Christians. Our love for God and others will cause us to put boundaries around our liberty. Though we may have the right, we also have the responsibility never to use our Christian liberty as a license to sin. The Bible never gives Christians permission to engage in sin. As Paul writes in 1 Corinthians 10:24, "Nobody should seek his own good, but the good of others." He clearly is not countenancing indulgence in sin. He has already countered that notion (Rom. 6:1). Sex, like food and everything physical, is temporal, not eternal, and destined to perish (1 Cor. 6:13). We are to live for the eternal.

With addictions, the substance, behavior, or thought has gained mastery over the lives of the addicts. They are not living selflessly or for the eternal. Jesus is not Lord; the addiction is lord. That leads to the logical conclusion that addictions are nothing less than idolatry—something or someone other than Jesus Christ has become lord in the life of that person. Something or someone other than the Lord God has become god. That is idolatry. That is a violation of the first of the Ten Commandments, "You shall have no other gods before me" (Exod. 20:3). The apostle Paul affirms that bondage to sexual immorality is idolatry when he warns the Ephesian church:

> But among you there must not be even a hint of sexual
> immorality, or of any kind of impurity, or of greed, because
> these are improper for God's holy people. Nor should there be
> obscenity, foolish talk or coarse joking, which are out of place,
> but rather thanksgiving. For of this you can be sure: No immoral,
> impure or greedy person—such a man is an idolater—has any
> inheritance in the kingdom of Christ and of God. (Eph. 5:3–5)

Using sexual immorality to seduce the people of God into deserting the one true God for idols is not new. This pattern was the prophet Balaam's counsel to King Balak (Num. 25:1–3, 31:15–18; Rev. 2:14). That same sexual immorality-idolatry connection is seen in 1 Corinthians 6:9–10 in which the apostle Paul lists the wicked who will not inherit the kingdom of God. In verse 9, the apostle names five categories of sexual sinners:

(a) the sexually immoral

(b) idolaters

(c) adulterers

(d) male prostitutes (literally "soft ones")

(e) homosexual offenders

In the midst of those committing sexual sins, the apostle lists "idolaters." His placement of idolaters in the context of sexual sins causes Morris to write, "The inclusion of *idolaters* may point us to the immorality of much heathen worship of the day."[67] Wiersbe adds, "In that day, idolatry and sensuality went together."[68] Some believe that Paul's use of "idolaters" in 1 Cor. 6:9 is a reference to the temple prostitutes serving the goddess Aphrodite in Corinth.[69]

We Become Like That Which We Worship

A sobering thought is that we become like that which we worship. If we worship the one true living God, we become like Him. If we worship an idol, we become like that idol. Consider the words of the psalmist:

---

[67] Morris, p. 97

[68] Wiersbe, p. 588.

[69] Findlay believes this to be the case. "*Idolaters* are ranged between *fornicators* and *adulterers*—an association belonging to the cultus of Aphrodite Pandemos at Corinth." Findlay, p. 817.

The idols of the nations are silver and gold, made by the hands
of men. They have mouths, but cannot speak, eyes, but they
cannot see; they have ears, but cannot hear, nor is there breath
in their mouths. Those who make them *will be like them*, and so
will all who trust in them. (Ps. 135:15–18, emphasis mine)

Those who have erected the idol of sex in their hearts become like
their idol. How they relate to themselves and others, their thoughts, words,
and actions, becomes sexual. Their thinking becomes distorted by the idol,
and sex is seen as their greatest need in life. That is exactly the thinking of the
sexually addicted. Dr. Patrick Carnes notes that one of the four core beliefs
of a sexual addict is, "Sex is my most important need."[70] The thinking of the
addict is, says Carnes, "I need sex all the time, cannot get enough, and must
not pass up any opportunities. I am the only one who needs sex this much."[71]
Those are the thoughts of one who has erected the idol of sex in his or her
heart.

Addiction Counseling Fails to Address the Sin of Idolatry

Much of today's addiction counseling fails to address the idolatry of
the addict. The focus is typically on symptom management instead of heart
transformation. Cessation of immoral behaviors is the primary goal of secular
addiction counseling, and the sexually addicted are rarely transformed. One of
the texts used in Sex Addicts Anonymous notes, "It is, after all, the Program
that keeps people sober … We are not recovered addicts; we are recovering
addicts."[72] Addicts are never free. They are always addicts, always bearing

---

[70] Carnes, *Out of the Shadows*, p.152.
[71] Ibid., p. 152.
[72] CompCare Publishers, *Hope & Recovery: A Twelve Step Guide to Healing
from Compulsive Sexual Behavior* (Minneapolis, MN: CompCare Publications, 1987), pp. 75, 76.

the label. The program (the 12 Step program of S.A.A.), not God, is given credit for enabling addicts to become sober. As Sex Addicts Anonymous says, "We know that the Program is the real miracle in all of this."[73] For those who name the name of Christ there is more. God transforms hearts and the Bible promises freedom from addictive behaviors. Jesus said, "So if the Son sets you free, you will be free indeed" (John 8:36). In Galatians 5:1–2, the apostle Paul writes, "It is for freedom that Christ has set us free. Stand firm, then, and do not let yourselves be burdened again by a yoke of slavery." The goal of the purity ministry is nothing less than heart transformation and freedom for those involved. The purity ministry desires every person to recover the true image of God in himself—one that is holy, pure in heart, free from sin, and passionately in love with Jesus Christ.

With regard to addictions, the goal of the secular addiction counselor is sexual sobriety and the cessation of the offending behavior. As good as it is, the goal of sobriety is inadequate. It fails to address the needs of the heart. Unless the heart is changed through true repentance and unless true intimacy with God and with one's spouse is achieved, changing thought patterns and behavioral responses will always fall short of God's desire for human beings. God's desire is not sobriety but for all people to reflect His glory. The reflection of God's glory through the inner transformation of the heart yields true freedom. Sobriety, while a good and necessary first step, is not a sufficient goal. A heart free from the desire to sexually sin is the only godly goal.

Medical Model

Many believe that sexual addiction is based on the medical or disease model of addictions. Research indicates that although physical predispositions

---

[73] Ibid., p. 127.

can push a person toward sexual addiction, that does not mean it is inevitable. Rather, sexual immorality and sexual addiction are attempts to meet legitimate needs for true intimacy in a sinful, self-willed way. Schaumburg is correct when he writes, "The biblical focus isn't on a disease that causes a problem but on humanity's deceitful heart that continues to create far greater problems than sexual dysfunction."[74] Under the biblical theory, sexual immorality is the fruit of a sinful heart in rebellion against God. Unless the heart problem is addressed, complete freedom will never be found—only sobriety. Sexual immorality requires a treatment plan as holistic as the problem. Because sexual immorality impacts body, soul, and spirit, all three parts of a person must be treated. Again Schaumburg reminds us, "If we see sexual addiction through the lens of the medical disease model, we drift into the trap of calling any destructive behavior an incurable ailment rather than a sin requiring the power of Christ for deliverance."[75]

The biblical approach to treating couples and individuals impacted by sexual immorality is the only approach that deals with the heart. Jesus said, in Matthew 5:28, "But I tell you that anyone who looks at a woman lustfully has already committed adultery with her in his heart." Sexual immorality affects the heart of a person. Because a defiled heart is the problem, a pure heart must be the solution. Jesus said, "Blessed are the pure in heart, for they will see God" (Matt. 5:8). Therefore, any treatment plan that fails to address the heart issue is only treating surface symptoms.

---

[74] Schaumburg, *False Intimacy,* p. 63.

[75] Ibid., p. 64.

CHAPTER FOUR
THE WAR ON PURITY

Then the dragon was enraged at the woman and went off to make war against the rest of her offspring—those who obey God's commandments and hold to the testimony of Jesus.

Revelation 12:17

Satan's War Against the Bride

The Origin of the War

The war began in eternity past. Satan and his rebel angels launched a coup against the Lord God and sought to dethrone Him and take over heaven. In Isaiah 14:12–17 and Ezekiel 28:12–19 we are presented with two glimpses into eternity past. Like most prophecy, there is a present and a distant fulfillment in each passage. In the Isaiah passage, the present fulfillment is Nebuchadnezzar, king of Babylon. Yet clearly the prophecy goes beyond Nebuchadnezzar to describe one who is "fallen from heaven ... down to the earth" (Isa. 14:12 NASV). This one is called the "star of the morning, son of the dawn." The Latin word used for "star of the morning" is Lucifer.

What started the war in heaven? Isaiah's prophecy gives us insight into the motivation for the war. Isaiah 14:12–14 tell us that five times Lucifer declared in his heart his intent to raise himself up to be co-equal with God. Five phrases, each beginning with "I will," describe the five aspects of God which Satan coveted. Each phrase provides insights into Satan's sin of pride. Satan desired:

(a) God's Place. From 14:13 ("I will ascend to heaven"), he coveted God's place in the third or highest heaven.

(b) God's Position. From 14:13 ("I will raise my throne above the stars of God"), Satan sought God's position as Ruler of the angels of heaven.

(c) God's Power. From 14:13 ("I will sit enthroned on the mount of assembly"), he coveted God's power as the Just Judge of all the universe.

(d) God's Presence. From 14:14 ("I will ascend above the tops of the clouds"), Satan sought God's glory.

(e) God's Person. From 14:14 ("I will make myself like the Most High"), Satan's ultimate purpose is to make himself co-equal with God, the fourth member of the godhead. Isaiah declares that because of his pride and self-willed aspirations, Satan was cast from heaven down to Sheol (OT "hell"). Satan's final estate is the lake of fire (Rev. 20:10). Thus, the sin of pride brought Satan condemnation (cf. 1 Tim. 3:6).

In the Ezekiel 28:12–19 passage, the present prophecy is directed at the king of Tyre (28:12); but, as with the Isaiah 14 passage, the message goes beyond this earthly king. We read of the purpose and splendor of Satan. Ezekiel presents six descriptors of Satan:

(a) Excellence. Satan was the greatest angel God had created. From 28:12 ("you were the model of perfection, full of wisdom and perfect in beauty"), Satan had God's seal upon him and was wise and beautiful.

(b) Access. From 28:13 ("you were in Eden, the garden of God"),

Satan had access to Eden.

(c) Beauty. From 28:13 we read of the jewel-bedecked robes Satan wore in his position as the covering cherub. They are similar to the twelve jewels embedded in the breastplate of the high priest of Israel (Exod. 28:17–20) and the twelve jewels in the foundation of the New Jerusalem (Rev. 21:19–20).

(d) Responsibility. From 28:14 ("you were anointed as a guardian cherub"), Satan had great responsibility and authority as the defender of God's holiness.

(e) Position. From 28:14 ("you were on the holy mount of God"), Satan had freedom to enter the very throne room of God at will.

(f) Holiness. From 28:15, Satan was holy and blameless prior to his fall into sin ("You were blameless in your ways ...").

As an angelic guardian of the throne, Satan was a member of the angelic order called the cherubim. Cherubim, Chafer says, were "the protectors and defenders of His holiness."[76] Thus, Satan is a created being, an angel, who originally was a protector of God's holiness. How can one who is described as "blameless" and "perfect" and a defender of God's holiness become the antithesis? Scripture refers to Satan's pride and unrighteousness as internal "violence" (28:16 NASV). Satan's pride led him to desire that which he could not attain, the throne of God. He began to slander God to the angels (28:16, "widespread trade"). It led to rebellion among the angels with some following Satan and some devoted to God. The outcome of the war was never in doubt. Satan and his rebel band of angels were cast down to earth (28:17).

---

[76] Chafer, *Systematic Theology*, p. II: 42.

The Attack on the First Adam and His Bride

The war was not over. It simply changed battlefields. Phase two of the war moved from heaven to Eden, the garden of God. When the theater of combat shifted from heaven to the garden, Satan focused his attack on the pinnacle of God's creation, human beings. Satan's strategy for attacking Adam and Eve utilized a combination of deception, lying, and "divide and conquer." It worked. First he attacked Adam's bride, Eve, through deception and lying, telling her, "You will not surely die. ... For God knows that when you eat of it your eyes will be opened, and you will be like God, knowing good and evil" (Gen. 3:4–5). Eve, in turn, gave the forbidden fruit to her husband who was with her (Gen. 3:6). Why didn't Satan attack Adam? Why did he attack Eve? By attacking Eve, Satan was able to defeat Adam. Why did Adam eat of the forbidden fruit? Surely he knew from whence it came. Several answers have been put forth for why Adam disobeyed God's command and ate of the fruit of the tree of the knowledge of good and evil:

(a) Love. Adam knew that Eve had disobeyed and would die, therefore, because of his knowledge of her sin, Adam ate the fruit choosing rather to die with the one he loved than to live without her. Sounds romantic but it is sheer conjecture.

(b) Willful disobedience. A second possible reason is that Adam heard Satan's words spoken to Eve because, according to Genesis 3:6, he was with her. He willfully chose to sin and disobey God. As the apostle Paul describes it, "For Adam was formed first, then Eve. And Adam was not the one deceived; it was the woman who was deceived and became a sinner" (1 Tim. 2:13–14). Adam was not deceived. He willfully chose to sin by disobeying God's command.

(c) Persuasion. Even as the serpent had persuaded Eve to eat of the fruit of the forbidden tree, so Eve persuaded Adam to eat of it.[77]

Regardless of why Adam disobeyed, it appears from the Genesis account that Adam was passive in the face of Satan's attack on his wife, Eve. He could have intervened at any time during the temptation and deception by Satan. He did not, even though, as Genesis 3:6 says, he "was with her." Was this passivity and failure to protect his bride unique to Adam and a onetime occurrence or is this a default pattern for humanity that transcends culture and time? Are we seeing this same pattern of male passivity and failure to protect women in our own culture today? We truly are of the sinful seed of Adam.

The Attack On The Second Adam and His Bride

Satan hates God and anything God loves. He attacked Jesus Christ, God's beloved one. By resurrecting Jesus, God defeated Satan. Now Satan, though defeated, turns his rage on the Bride of the Second Adam, the Church. Satan reasons that the strategy of attacking the bride in the garden of Eden worked to cause the first Adam to sin. So he attacks Christians, the Bride of the Second Adam.

He not only attacks Christians in the hope of causing them to sin and be disqualified to be Christ's Bride, but he attacks them because they are indwelt by God's Spirit. Revelation 12:17 declares, "Then the dragon was enraged at the woman and went off to make war against the rest of her offspring—those who obey God's commandments and hold to the testimony of Jesus."

D-Day For Satan

The final phase of the war is recorded in Revelation 20:8–10 as

---

[77] Flavius Josephus, *The Antiquities of the Jews* in *Josephus: Complete Words* (Grand Rapids, MI: Kregel Publications, 1981), p. 26.

Satan, following the millennium, leads a last ditch effort to crush the saints of God and the holy city of Jerusalem where Jesus rules. He is defeated and thrown into the lake of fire with the other members of the "unholy trinity," the beast and the false prophet (cf. Matt. 25:41). Jesus and His Bride reign supreme!

The Enemies of Purity

Satan is Purity Enemy Number One

Who are the enemies of purity? Who wants to defile the Bride? Let's start with Satan. We've already talked a lot about him. Here's a recap. Satan hates Christ and, because the Church is indwelt by the Spirit of Christ and embodies Christ on the earth, Satan hates the Church. Satan wants to destroy her any way he can. Sexual sin is one of his most potent weapons for destroying the Church. Satan's strategy of using sexual sin to destroy the Church is not new. He has been using sexual sin to destroy God's people for millennia. Whether it was the incest of the daughters of Lot with their father, the adultery of King David with Bathsheba, the rape of Tamar by Amnon, the polygamy of Solomon, or the Corinthian man who committed adultery with his stepmother, sexual sin has been the common denominator Satan has used to bring death and heartache. Remember Balaam's counsel to King Balak? Balaam counseled Balak to use sexual sin to lure Israel into idolatry and defeat (Num. 25:1–5). The New Testament commentary on Numbers 25:1–5 identifies the role of sexual sin in the death of 24,000 Israelites when it says, "We should not commit sexual immorality as some of them did …" (1 Cor. 10:8).

Satan uses sexual immorality with the goal of rendering the Bride unclean, defiled, and unfit to marry. After all, the law of God clearly stated that a priest could not marry a defiled woman who was not a virgin (Lev. 21:13–14). Jesus Christ is a high priest according to the order of Melchizedek (Heb. 7:1–28), and if the Levitical priests could not defile themselves by marrying an impure woman, how much more must Christ not marry an impure, defiled one?

The World Around Us

We live in a sexualized world. We see it reflected in our western culture. Sex is used to sell everything from beer to minivans. Television routinely broadcasts advertisements for erectile dysfunction medications and male enhancement products. Sexualization is not limited to the United States. It is a global phenomenon. In Europe, tabloids print photos displaying full frontal nudity to sell newspapers. The storefront prostitutes of Amsterdam are infamous. China, South Korea, and Japan have become the leading consumers of pornography. Human trafficking and sexual slavery are on the rise as predators buy and sell children and teens for sexual purposes. We live in a sexualized world.

The world is enemy number two. What do we mean by that? The English term "world" has several meanings including:

(a) the humans inhabiting the planet (John 3:16)

(b) the planet (1 Cor. 5:10)

(c) the satanic, godless value system embraced by lost people on the planet (James 4:4) The New Testament uses three different Greek words to translate our word *world*:

(a) αἰών [*aiōn*] (English word "eon"), meaning "time, age" as in Matthew 28:20 (NASV), "… and lo, I am with you always, even to the end of the age"

(b) οἰκουμένη [*oikoumenē*] (English word "ecumenical"), meaning "inhabited earth, nations" as in Matthew 24:14, "And this gospel of the kingdom will be preached in the whole world as a testimony to all nations, and then the end will come"

(c) κόσμος [*kosmos*] (English word "cosmos"), meaning "world system" as in Matthew 5:14, "You are the light of the world. A city on a hill cannot be hidden." Kosmos is used 186 times in the New Testament making it the primary word translated "world." Kosmos is the opposite of chaos. Kosmos means a system or order determined by a mastermind.[78] Satan is that mastermind.

How did the world gain the sexual values it espouses? Through Satan. Satan is the "god of this world" (2 Cor. 4:4 NASV). He rules this world, says Matthew 4:8–9, and its values reflect his values. The Bible says that Christians are not to love the world or embrace its values (1 John 2:15–17, James 4:4–5). To befriend the world, that is to embrace its values and make them our own, instantly makes us enemies of God, says James 4:4! We cannot claim to belong to God and yet live for the world. We cannot serve two masters (Matt. 6:24).

The Flesh: The Enemy Within

The flesh is our third enemy. Like the term *world*, "flesh" can have several meanings. We could be talking about the skin on our bodies, our flesh (Luke 24:39) or the sinful nature we inherited from Adam. Again, the New

---

[78]   Chafer, p. 180.

Testament Greek uses two different words to translate flesh:

(a) σῶμα [sōma], (English "somatic") meaning "body"

(b) σάρξ [sarx] meaning "the sin nature within every human

being."[79]

Arndt and Gingrich define flesh as "the willing instrument of sin."[80]

It is our flesh which desires to sin. The apostle John speaks of it as the "lust

of the flesh" (1 John 2:16 NASV). In many ways, we are our own worst enemy.

Our flesh desires to sexually sin. It is the enemy within.

The Strategy of the Enemy

The Enemy's Strategy: Temptation.

One of the names used to describe Satan is "tempter" (Matt. 4:3,

1 Thess. 3:5). He tempts people to sin by acting independently of God.

That is how he tempted Eve. He approached her with two temptations. The

first temptation was to question God's word. Satan asked, "Did God really

say, 'You must not eat from any tree in the garden'?" (Gen. 3:1). Satan is

insinuating that God's word is open for discussion, debate, or interpretation.

Perhaps his intent in questioning Eve is to cause her to doubt herself as to

what God actually said. "He cannot mean what you think He means," Satan

implies. All temptation begins with questioning the standard of God's word.

The second temptation was to question God's love. Satan boldly states, "You

will not surely die... (Gen. 3:4). "God is a liar. God is withholding good from

you. God does not really love you. If He did, He would never have restricted

your freedom to eat," is the force of his words.

And so a deceived and possibly confused Eve acts independently of

---

[79] Ibid., p. 183.
[80] Arndt & Gingrich, p. 751.

God and disobeys the protective prohibition of God. As mentioned before, Adam passively stood by and let Satan attack his wife. He was not deceived (1 Tim. 2:14). He knowingly, deliberately, willfully disobeyed God and ate the fruit of the tree of the knowledge of good and evil.

Satan has used that same approach to tempt multiplied generations of men and women since he succeeded with the first couple. Questioning God's word leads to questioning God's love. If we believe the first lie, invariably we believe the second. If we question God's word, it is a short step until we question His love.

The three primary vehicles of temptation.

In 1 John 2:15–17, we are told not to love the world or the things of the world. The world is the enemy of God (cf. James 4:4). The Bible goes on to describe the three primary ways we love the world: "the lust of the flesh," "the lust of the eyes," and "the boastful pride of life" (NASV). These same three are the vehicles of temptation Satan used in Eden with Eve. Eve "saw that the tree was good for food" (Gen. 3:6 NASV) thus arousing the lust of the flesh. The lust of the flesh is the desire to meet legitimate bodily needs in an illegitimate way. Lust is the ungodly sense of the word *desire*.[81] Lust is the sinful desire of the heart.

Eve then saw that the tree was "a delight to the eyes" (Gen. 3:6 NASV). Now the lust of the eyes is aroused. Eve's flesh not only craves the fruit, but so do her eyes. She sees the beauty and uniqueness of it. The lust of the eyes is the desire to visually "snack" on legitimate beauty in an illegitimate way. The eye becomes the portal for temptation to lust after the

---

[81] ἐπιθυμία [*epithumia*] "desire, longing." Can be used in a good, neutral, or bad sense. Used in a bad sense, ἐπιθυμία, is translated as "lust." Arndt & Gingrich, p. 293.

forbidden food.

Finally, Eve understands that the fruit of the tree "was desirable to make one wise" (Gen. 3:6 NASV). Satan uses the fruit to tempt her to become wise. He appeals to her "pride of life." She reasons to herself, "Doesn't everyone want to be wise? What is wrong with being wise?" The boastful pride of life is the desire for legitimate wisdom gained in an illegitimate way. Wisdom is discerning between good and evil, not simply knowing good and evil. Wisdom is a mark of the mature (Heb. 5:14).

Sexual temptation.

Knowing that the Lord God has declared sexuality as very good, Satan attacks it with a vengeance. How does he tempt us in the area of sexuality? He tempts us to meet our legitimate need for sexual intimacy in illegitimate ways. He tempts us to disobey the sexual protections set forth in the law (Lev. 18–22), the writings (Prov. 5–7), the gospels (Matt. 5:19), the epistles (1 Cor. 6–7), and written in our consciences. Again, the definition of sin is to live independently of God. That is Satan's goal.

He uses the same three vehicles to tempt us sexually that he used with Eve in the garden. He uses sex to appeal to our flesh. He tempts us to meet the legitimate need for sexual intimacy through illegitimate ways. He tempts us to defy God's protective prohibitions. He wants us to question God's word, "Why can't I meet my need for sex outside of marriage?" He then provokes us to question God's love, "If God really loved me, He'd let me enjoy sex any way I choose to express it. He must not love me because He's restricting my freedom. I know better than God how to meet my needs."

The legitimate use of our eyes is to have an altruistic appreciation of God's creation. God made all things beautiful in their way. Satan tempts us to use our eyes to desire beauty illegitimately. He tempts us to covet it. Job declared, "I made a covenant with my eyes not to look lustfully at a girl" (Job 31:1). Satan tempts us to lust with our eyes by visually consuming beauty in illegitimate ways. Satan wants us to use our eyes to look, not as an appreciator, but as a consumer. He provokes us to think, "I'd like to see more skin. I wish I could see her naked. I wonder what he looks like without his shirt on. I can use my eyes to look at anything I choose. I am lord over my eyes." All of that is the lust of the eyes. Once again, Satan tempts us to question God's word and God's love. Jesus prohibited such use of our eyes when He said, "You have heard that it was said, 'Do not commit adultery.' But I tell you that anyone who looks at a woman lustfully has already committed adultery with her in his heart" (Matt. 5:27–28). The lust of the eyes is adultery of the heart.

Finally, Satan tempts us in our pride. He tempts us to boast of our sexual conquests. He tempts us to satisfy our legitimate desire for wisdom on sexuality in illegitimate ways such as viewing pornography. He provokes us to think, "I need to know more sexually. I need to be knowledgeable. I don't want to go into marriage and have my spouse think I'm an inexperienced lover. He/she might leave me." And so we question God's word and His love. God tells us to confine our sexuality to marriage in order to protect us. God loves us and knows what is best for His children. He created marriage and gave it as a gift to mankind. We resist the "shackles" of His protection and see them as restrictive to our freedom.

Satan the accuser.

Once we have yielded to his temptation and sinned, Satan then becomes the "accuser of our brothers" (Rev. 12:10).[82] He accuses us to God and to ourselves. As he did with Job, Satan has access to the throne of God to accuse us (Job 1:6–12, 2:1-6). As Christians, we have a defender, the Lord Jesus Christ. He is our Advocate (1 Tim. 2:5, Luke 22:31–32). He pleads our case before the Father (1 John 2:1). So with the one hand Satan tempts us to sin and with the other he accuses us to God and ourselves when we do. Satan whispers to us, "How can you call yourself a Christian when you sexually sin like that? You must not be a Christian at all." Were it not for our Advocate, Jesus Christ, we would be lost indeed. Our defense is not found in pointing to our righteousness but His. He is the sinless one. He is the righteous one. He is our great High Priest (Heb. 7:25–26). In Him we stand faultless before the throne of God (Col. 3:3).

What is at Stake in the War?

The attack on the Bride is relentless. Satan does not quit. What is at stake? The purity of the Bride is at stake. That is no small thing. Listen to the words of Harry Schaumberg, a therapist who has been treating sexual addiction for over twenty-eight years, "I believe this colossal, moral-ethical-behavioral shift to self-stimulated, self-centered, and impersonal sex is putting the Church in the most consequential, spiritual-moral crisis in the history of Western culture."[83] The out-of-control sexuality seen in the West is a harbinger of the coming moral collapse of our culture.

---

[82] I am indebted to Dr. Neil T. Anderson for his insights into the dual strategy of temptation-accusation used by the devil. This is explained in his book, *The Bondage Breaker* (Eugene, OR: Harvest House Publishers, 1990), pp. 125-151.

[83] Harry Schaumberg, "False Intimacy and Sexual Addiction: A Modern Epidemic," *Christian Counseling Today,* 1, 14, p. 25.

CHAPTER FIVE
THE ENEMY'S WEAPON OF SEXUAL IMMORALITY

For though we live in the world, we do not wage war as the world does. The weapons we fight with are not the weapons of the world. On the contrary, they have divine power to demolish strongholds.

2 Corinthians 10:3–4

The Primary Weapon of the Enemy

The three primary enemies of purity which attack Christians and would, if possible, defile them and render them spiritually impure are Satan, the world, and the flesh. What weapons does our enemy use to attack the Church?

Sexual Immorality Is Porneia

Although there are three enemies which Christians battle, our primary focus is on Satan because he is the architect of evil and the commander-in-chief of the enemies of God. Satan plans the attacks and uses the world for his purposes. What weapons does our enemy use in the war for purity? He has many at his disposal but his primary weapon is the temptation to become sexually immoral.

73

As we saw in chapter three, sexual immorality (πορνεία [*porneia*]) is a broad, umbrella term for sexual sin that spans the spectrum from legal sexual sins such as fornication and adultery to illegal sexual sins such as rape and incest (see "Sexual Interaction Table" in chapter 1). All are sexual sins. All are forms of sexual immorality. The difference is not in degrees of sinfulness but rather in dependency, violence, and legality. Sexual immorality is "every kind of unlawful sexual intercourse."[84]

When Sexual Sin Becomes Sexual Addiction

If sexual immorality is the umbrella term for all manner of sexual sin, what is sexual addiction and what's the difference between sexual sin and sexual addiction? When does sexual sin cross the line into sexual addiction?

As mentioned in chapter one, not all sexual sinners are sexual addicts but all sexual addicts are sexual sinners. Sexual addiction is a form of bondage. Sexual sin crosses the line into sexual addiction when we purpose to quit, but can't stop doing it. It has gained mastery over us. Although the Bible never uses the terms "addict" or "addiction," it does use several synonymous terms: "mastery," "bondage," "lordship," and "slavery." All addictions are forms of slavery. As discussed in chapter three, all addictions are also forms of idolatry. Consider the apostle Paul's words:

> "Everything is permissible for me" — but not everything is beneficial. "Everything is permissible for me"—but I will not be mastered by anything. Food for the stomach and the stomach for

---

[84] Arndt & Gingrich, pp. 699; Hauck, F., & Schulz, S. (1982). πόρνη, πόρνος, πορνεία, πορνεύω, ἐκπορνεύω, In Gerhard Kittel, & G. Friedrich (Eds.), *Theological Dictionary of the New Testament* (G. W. Bromiley, Trans., Vol. 6) (Grand Rapids, MI: William B. Eerdmans Publishing Company), pp. 579-595.

food—but God will destroy them both. The body is not meant for sexual immorality, but for the Lord. and the Lord for the body" (1 Cor. 6:12–13).

Nothing and no one but Jesus Christ is to master us (Rom. 6:14, 10:9, 1 Cor. 12:3, Phil. 2:11).

Four Clear Evidences of Sexual Addiction

Although there are many characteristics of sexual addiction, Schaumberg lists the following four clear evidences:

(a) Compelling and consuming behavior. For the sexual addict, sex becomes his greatest need—not greatest desire. Sex is wanted, demanded, and will be pursued at any cost.

(b) Behavior leading to negative consequences. Sexually transmitted diseases (STDs), loss of career, spouse, family, reputation, financial ruin, shame, etc. are all negative consequences of sexual addictio

(c) Out-of-control behavior. Lacking "willpower," addicts feel unable to stop craving, using, thinking about, or caring about sexual behavior even when they know their behavior is harmful and want to stop.

(d) Denial of the behavior's seriousness. Sex addicts often deny that their behavior is out of control and that bad experiences are occurring as a result of the addictive behavior.[85]

Sexual addiction is dependency upon a sinful sexual behavior to meet personal needs. A sexual behavior becomes an addiction when it gains mastery over a person and the person is dependent upon it. Regardless of whether or not his or her life has become unmanageable, he or she cannot stop the behavior. Sexual addiction is a "pathological relationship to any form of

---

[85] Schaumburg, *False Intimacy,* pp. 22, 23.

sexual activity."[86]

Is sexual addiction the same as sexual compulsion? The answer is yes, since both terms are used interchangeably. Carnes objects to the use of the term sexual compulsion. He prefers the term sexual addiction to describe those who abuse sex. He writes, "There are some who see the problem clearly but hesitate to call it an addiction. They choose words like 'compulsive' or 'hypersexual'—yet they have absolutely no problem calling compulsive gambling an addiction."[87]

In the psychological community, sexual addiction is often used synonymously with the term sexual obsession. The implication is that sexual addiction is primarily a mental illness. Is sexual addiction a mental illness? Although the DSM-IV (1994) has no specific category for sexual addiction, something that Carnes and others are seeking to rectify in the DSM-V, it does indicate that obsession in the form of sexual imagery may indicate obsessive-compulsive disorder. The DSM-IV says:

> Obsessions are persistent ideas, thoughts, impulses, or images
> that are experienced as intrusive and inappropriate and that
> cause marked anxiety or distress. The intrusive and inappropriate
> quality of the obsessions has been referred to as "ego-dystonic"
> This refers to the individual's sense that the content of the
> obsession is alien, not within his or her own control, and not the

---

[86]   Ralph Earle & Mark Laaser, *The Pornography Trap: Setting Pastors and Laypersons Free from Sexual Addiction* (Kansas City, MO: Beacon Hill Press of Kansas City, 2002), p. 12.
[87]   Carnes, *Don't Call it Love: Recovery from Sexual Addiction* (New York, NY: Bantam Books, 1992), p. 10.

kind of thought that he or she would expect to have.[88]

Sexual Addiction Differs from Normal Sexual Desire

What differentiates sexual addiction from normal sexual desire? Arterburn and Stoeker write, "It's easy to confuse normal sexual desire and conduct with addictive compulsions and gratification. A person can have a stronger-than-normal sexual appetite and not be a sex addict."[89] Arterburn goes on to list seven differences between sexual addiction and normal sexual desire:

(a) Addictive sex is done in isolation and is devoid of relationship. Addictive sex is "mere sex," sex for its own sake, sex divorced from authentic interaction of persons.

(b) Addictive sex is secretive.

(c) Addictive sex is devoid of intimacy.

(d) Addictive sex is victimizing.

(e) Addictive sex ends in despair.

(f) Addictive sex is used to escape pain and problems.

(g) Like any addiction, addictive sex is progressive.[90]

The following table is helpful in comparing sex addicts and non-sex addicts.

[88] American Psychiatric Association, *Diagnostic and Statistical Manual of Mental Disorders* (Washington, DC: American Psychiatric Association, 1994), p. 418.

[89] Stephen Arterburn & Fred Stoeker, *Every Man's Battle: Winning the War on Sexual Temptation One Victory at a Time* (Colorado Springs, CO: Waterbrook Press, 2000), p. 28.

[90] Ibid., pp. 28, 29.

The Differences Between Sex Addicts and Non-Sex Addicts[91]

Behaviors and Thoughts	Sex Addicts	Non-Sex Addicts
Thinks about sex	Constantly	Occasionally
Encounters sexual stimuli, such as pornography or an attractive person	Initiates a cycle of sexual thoughts and hope-for sexual activities. Disregards all moral and spiritual boundaries.	Notes the stimulus and moves on to other thoughts. Considers all moral and spiritual boundaries.
Masturbation	Becomes a habitual pattern used to medicate feelings.	Experiments but doesn't allow it to become a pattern.
Experience of sexual sin	Goes through a cycle of guilt and shame but repeats the sin.	Repents, confesses, and learns from the experience.
Marital sexuality	Selfish use of spouse to meet needs, including the need to avoid feelings.	Selfless expression of the deepest levels of emotional and spiritual intimacy.

Causes of Sexual Addiction

Sexual addiction is a multi-causal problem requiring a multi-dimensional approach to treatment. The origin of the problem is both internal and external. Pornography, masturbation, sexual fantasies, hiring prostitutes, etc., are the surface level behaviors indicating deeper issues. If the focus is primarily on stopping surface level behaviors but little effort is made to address the deeper issues of the addict, the addiction will continue. The sexual addict may return to his addiction or his addiction may resurface in another form. In fact, most sex addicts have "addiction interaction disorder" having concurrent addictions. Laaser says, "The average sexual addict has at least one other addiction. When one doesn't work, he flips into the other addiction. 50 percent of all sex addicts are chemically dependent. 33 percent have eating disorders. 50 percent of all alcoholics are sex addicts. 80 percent

---

[91] Laaser, *Healing the Wounds*, p. 27.

of all cocaine addicts are sex addicts."[92] Many clinicians have identified pornography, masturbation, and sexual fantasy as three of the major behaviors leading to sexual addiction. These three are often known as "building-block behaviors," because they are foundational behaviors upon which the sexual addict builds his or her addiction. These three sexual behaviors combine to begin a vicious cycle in the addict. Pornography fuels lust which, in turn, compels masturbation. Masturbation reinforces pornographic images in the mind resulting in sexual fantasizing. Sexual fantasy drives the addict back to pornography for another "fix." Without intervention in the cycle, the addict is trapped. All three building blocks will be addressed in this book but pornography is the sole subject of chapter six.

External Causes

What are the causes of sexual addiction? Is sexual addiction inherited from one's family-of-origin, caused by choices made in response to one's environment, or a spiritual attack of Satan? The external causes are many and varied.

Family-of-origin causes of sexual addiction.

Most sexual addiction therapists recognize that the family-of-origin plays a part in sexual addiction. Laaser states, "Sexual addiction begins in unhealthy families."[93] Unhealthy families bear out a number of characteristics: 1. Abuse. Unhealthy families tend to be abusive and wound one another. Abuse of a child or adult is included in the DSM-IV and is considered a "V"

---

[92] Laaser, *Treating the Addicted and Dysfunctional Family System* (Paper presented at Denver Seminary, Denver, CO, January 16-19, 2001). On the polyaddictive nature of sexual addiction also see Patrick Carnes, *Out of the Shadows,* p. 8.

[93] Mark Laaser, *Faithful & True: Sexual Integrity in a Fallen World* (Grand Rapids, MI: Zondervan Publishing House, 1996), p.79.

code.[94] Abuse in a family leads to a wounded child. That wounding may take the form of active abuse or passive abuse, often called neglect. With active abuse, aggression is perpetrated on the victim. With passive abuse, the victim is neglected or deprived of what they should rightfully receive. Abuse may be physical, sexual, emotional, or spiritual. Examples of active physical abuse of a child are beating, slapping, punching, burning, biting, kicking, and shoving. Active sexual abuse may take the form of inappropriate touching, incest, or rape. Examples of passive physical abuse of a child include physical neglect, inadequate supervision, not receiving good touches, not being hugged, kissed, embraced, or cuddled. Passive sexual abuse may involve never seeing sexuality modeled well by the parents or incomplete or absent sexual information. Active emotional abuse involves shaming statements, cutting or belittling remarks, and angry remarks. Active emotional wounds strike at the very core of a person's identity and self-worth. They make one feel inferior, insecure, stupid, worthless, or unwanted. Active emotional abuse can take the form of sexual abuse when a child views parental nudity or pornography or hears sexual jokes, sexual stories, or sexual remarks being spoken. Passive emotional abuse is just as damaging as active though less obvious. Passive emotional wounds come from being ignored or not being told what should have been told. All of us should have been told: "I love you," "you are wanted," "you are so good at (sport, hobby, academic, etc.)," "I'm so glad you are our son/daughter and part of our family." Passive emotional wounds come from fathers or mothers who are emotionally cold, distant, uncaring, absent, or simply silent. As Eldredge says, "Some fathers give a wound merely by their

---

[94] American Psychiatric Association, *DSM-IV,* p. 682.

silence; they are present, yet absent to their sons. The silence is deafening."[95] With passive emotional wounds a child does not get the affirmation, nurturing, and love he or she should have gotten.

Finally, active spiritual abuse is when parents use the Bible, church, or God as weapons to control or force children to conform to standards or expectations. Phrases such as: "God doesn't like you when you behave this way," "The Bible says (quotation from Bible) and you'd better obey or else," and "you call yourself a Christian. Christians don't (think, behave, feel) like that." Active spiritual wounds can also come from becoming angry with God or blaming God for disappointments, unmet needs, or unfulfilled expectations. Satanic Ritual Abuse (SRA) or cultic ritual abuse are both forms of active spiritual abuse. Passive spiritual abuse comes when a child does not receive the spiritual training or opportunities for spiritual growth he or she should have received. The child who is never prayed with at bedtime, never taken to Sunday School or church, never read to from the Bible, never given the opportunity to receive Jesus Christ personally are all forms of passive spiritual abuse.

2. Poor boundaries. Unhealthy families tend to have either rigid boundaries or too-loose boundaries. Boundary violations lead to abuse. Boundaries define a person's space and help them feel safe and protected. When boundaries are too loose, doors are open that should be closed, and individual privacy is transgressed. Loose boundaries produce conditions ripe for sexual violations

---

[95] John Eldredge, *Wild at Heart: Discovering the Secret of a Man's Soul* (Nashville, TN: Thomas Nelson Publishers, 2001), p. 71.

such as incest to take place.[96]

When boundaries are too rigid the good that should happen doesn't. Good words, good touches, good feelings do not occur. Everyone is starved for affection and attention.

3. Unreasonable rules. Unhealthy families tend to have family rules which are unreasonable and often unspoken: don't talk, don't feel, and don't trust. If family members have an issue with how the family is being led or with someone's addiction in the family, the understood rule is, "we don't talk about that." If someone in the family feels anger, disappointment, or hurt, the rule is, "don't feel that way." Family members are unconsciously encouraged to internalize their feelings ("stuffing"). In the dysfunctional family system members don't trust one another. In addition when problems arise, family members tend to minimize, deny, or blame them on others. Personal responsibility for problems is seldom accepted.

4. Roles. They have roles to play. Family members in both healthy and unhealthy families play roles. Those roles are the parts each member plays in the family system. Family roles can include:

(a) the hero

(b) the scapegoat

(c) the mascot

(d) the lost child

(e) the little prince/princess

(f) the enabler

---

[96] Henry Cloud, H., & John Townsend, J., *Boundaries in Marriage* (Grand Rapids, MI: Zondervan Publishing House, 1999); Laaser, *Healing,* pp. 76-79.

(g) the dependent

(h) the saint.[97]

Satan is an external cause of addiction.

Probably the least often considered cause of sexual addiction is Satan. The Bible calls Satan the "tempter" who roams the earth "like a roaring lion looking for someone to devour" (Matt. 4:3, 1 Pet. 5:8). Satan is actively engaged in tempting people in the area of their greatest vulnerability. For many that area is sex. Satan desires the worship and adoration that rightly belong to Almighty God alone. Denied that, he seeks to enslave people through addictions, especially sexual addiction. He tempts men and women with the "forbidden fruit" of sex outside the protective boundaries of marriage. When men and women succumb to his temptations, the "death cycle" begins (cf. James 1:13–15).

Relational causes of sexual addiction.

Many men seek out pornography because it is easier to fill their hearts with false intimacy than making the effort and risking the vulnerability of true intimacy with their wives. The fear of rejection, vulnerability, and ridicule drives many to take the path of least resistance and effort. Eldredge puts it this way:

> What makes pornography so addictive is that more than
> anything else in a lost man's life, it makes him *feel* like a
> man without ever requiring a thing of him. The less a guy
> feels like a real man in the presence of a real woman, the
> more vulnerable he is to porn.[98]

---

[97] Laaser, *Faithful & True,* pp. 87-92; Gary J. Oliver, *Treating the Addicted and Dysfunctional Family System Class Notes* (Paper presented at Denver Seminary, Denver, CO, January 16-19, 2001).

[98] Eldredge, p. 44.

Schaumberg feels that sexual addiction has as its primary goal the avoidance of relational pain. He says, "In effect, a sex addict creates a pseudo relationship with something or someone who can be controlled, such as a picture, an actor on the video screen, or a prostitute."[99] Whether it is pornography, masturbation, sexual fantasy, prostitution, voyeurism, or any other sexual sin, the sex addict is pursuing false intimacy by way of sinful behavior rather than true intimacy with God and his or her spouse. Why? There are many reasons including:

(a) fear

(b) laziness

(c) family-of-origin modeling

(d) ignorance

(e) selfishness

(f) defective character development, and, most significantly

(g) sin

Sin is "autonomy from God."[100] It is a failure to depend on Him and a reliance on self to meet needs. Sin is living independently of God. That is what the sex addict is doing—attempting to get his or her need for intimacy met independent of a relationship with God or spouse. The sex addict chooses to avoid true intimacy and settles for "the passing pleasures of sin" (Heb. 11:25 NASV). Just as sinful choices got the addict addicted in the first place, so godly choices are the path to healing and freedom.

Internal Causes

Physical causes of sexual addiction.

The first of the physical causes of sexual addiction we will consider is the

---

[99] Schaumburg, p. 20.

[100] Ibid., p. 60.

biochemical factor. Science is making amazing discoveries about the human brain. We now know that neurochemicals produced in the brain can stimulate and elevate mood. Reisman explains, "we now know that emotionally arousing images imprint and alter the brain, triggering an instant, involuntary, but lasting, biochemical memory trail. This applies to so-called 'soft-core' and 'hard-core' pornography."[101] Three of the major biochemicals triggered in the body by viewing pornography are adrenalin (epinephrine), testosterone, and dopamine. Testosterone and dopamine are called androgens. Androgens are sex hormones and produce sexual excitatory action. The androgens very quickly increase sexual desire and sexual thoughts and fantasies.[102]

When pornography is viewed, adrenalin is secreted by the adrenal glands. Adrenalin is called the "fight or flight" drug. Regarding adrenalin, Milkman & Sunderwirth write:

> Hans Selye introduced the concept of getting high on our own stress hormones. When we become excited, either through anger or fear, the brain signals hormone-producing glands to release chemicals that prepare us for fight or flight. The adrenal glands produce cortisol, a chemical that increases blood sugar and speeds up the body's metabolism. Other messages to the adrenal glands result in the release of the amphetamine-like stimulant epinephrine (adrenalin), which helps supply glucose to the muscles and brain, and

---

[101]   Judith A. Reisman, *Hearing on the Brain Science Behind Pornography Addiction and the Effects of Addiction on Families and Communities*. (Washington, DC: U. S. Senate Committee on Commerce, Science & Transportation, November 18, 2004).

[102]   Lenore T. Szuchman & Frank Muscarella (Eds.), *Psychological Perspectives on Human Sexuality* (New York, NY: John Wiley & Sons, Inc., 2000), p. 69.

norepinephrine, which speeds up the heart rate and elevates blood pressure.[103]

Any sexual stimulant, whether viewing pornography, masturbating, sexual fantasizing, or anticipating cybersex, acts as a stressor to the body thus inducing the secretion of adrenalin.

Scientists refer to adrenalin as epinephrine. Epinephrine is released in response to trauma. Epinephrine causes the brain to lock the traumatic image into long-term memory. Normal, non-traumatic images that don't trigger the release of epinephrine are stored in short-term memory. The brain treats pornography as a form of trauma releasing epinephrine and storing the images and messages in long-term memory. This explains the difficulty those who have been exposed to pornography have with erasing the images from their memories. It also reinforces the necessity for Christians to "flee sexual immorality" (1 Cor. 6:18) and to have our minds renewed by the Word of God (Rom. 12:2).[104]

Testosterone is present in males and, to a minute degree, in females. Testosterone is produced in the Leydig cells of the testes. Testosterone is responsible for, among other things, further growth and adult sexual differentiation. During puberty in boys, the testes increase in size, the penis grows thicker and longer, pubic hair and body hair start to appear, and lowering of the voice begins. Testosterone also sensitizes the brain to initiate and to sustain the sexual response. Testosterone affects sexual

---

[103] Harvey B. Milkman & Stanley G. Sunderwirth, *Craving for Ecstasy: The Consciousness and Chemistry of Escape* (Lexington, MA: D. C. Heath and Company, 1987), pp. 95-97.
[104] Jane Brody, "Cybersex Leads to Psychological Disorder" (*New York Times News Service, May 22, 2000)*, pp. 1-33; James L. McGaugh, *Making and Preserving Memories* (Retrieved July 20, 2005, from http://www.ihf.org/lecture/mcgaugh3_trans.html#top, 2003).

desire. Testosterone encourages men to engage in risky sexual behavior. In a number of studies, testosterone appeared to be necessary for cognitive sexual functioning (fantasy, sexual daydreaming [fantasy], the experience of desire).[105]

Dopamine, another androgen, "increases the likelihood of erections in normal males and in men with psychogenic erectile dysfunction."[106] Dopamine elevates a person's mood. As an androgen, it increases the number of excitatory neurotransmitter molecules in the synapses of the brain, thus increasing excitement. Produced by the brain in several areas of the brain including the prefrontal cortex, dopamine produces the same pleasurable effects on the body as an opiate (such as morphine or heroin). As Satinover observes, "modern science allows us to understand that the underlying nature of an addiction to pornography is chemically nearly identical to a heroin addiction: Only the delivery system is different, and the sequence of steps."[107]

In his classic study, James Olds established the existence of "pleasure centers" in the brain. Electrodes were implanted in various regions of the brains of rats and were wired so that a rat could stimulate its own brain by pressing a lever. When the electrodes were placed in certain regions—in particular, the septal region and the hypothalamus—the rats would press the lever thousands of times per hour and would forego food and sleep and endure pain in order to stimulate these regions.[108]

---

[105] James Dobson, *Bringing Up Boys* (Wheaton, IL: Tyndale House Publishers, 2001), pp. 19-23; Hyde & DeLamater, p. 117, 118; Szuchman & Muscarella, pp. 69-71.

[106] Szuchman & Muscarella, p. 70.

[107] Jeffrey Satinover, *Hearing on the Brain Science behind Pornography Addiction and the Effects of Addiction on Families and Communities* (Washington, DC: U. S. Senate Committee on Commerce, Science, and Transportation, November 18, 2004).

[108] James Olds, "Pleasure Centers in the Brain" (*Scientific American , 193*,

Carnes notes:

We have learned that addictive obsession can exist in

whatever generates significant mood alteration, whether it

is the self-nurturing of food, the excitement of gambling, or

the arousal of seduction. One of the more destructive parts

of sex addiction is that you literally carry your own source

of supply."[109]

Masturbation.

Masturbation, one of the three building-block behaviors, can become an addictive behavior. It is the second of the physical causes for sexual addiction. Typically begun during pre-adolescence, masturbation escalates in frequency reaching its peak period during middle adolescence. According to an NHSLS (National Health and Social Life Survey) conducted by Edward Laumann, 63 percent of men and 42 percent of women report masturbating during the past year. Masturbation is a mood-altering behavior. It creates a feeling of euphoria. By climaxing in orgasm, masturbation becomes a substitute for sexual intercourse. For many sexual addicts, masturbation is a compulsive behavior that is done four to five times per day. It becomes part of their secret life.[110]

Masturbation is not an issue of concern for secular sex therapists. Learning to masturbate privately and as a couple is a standard behavioral reconditioning intervention in sex therapy. Masturbation is not seen as morally

---

1956), pp. 105-116; Hyde & DeLamater, p. 241.

[109] Patrick Carnes, *Don't Call it Love: Recovery from Sexual Addiction* (New York, NY: Bantam Books, 1992), p. 30.

[110] Laaser, 2004, pp. 33-35; Hyde & DeLamater, pp. 293-296; Edward O. Laumann et al., *The social Organization of Sexuality: Sexual Practices in the United States* (Chicago, IL: University of Chicago Press, 1994).

wrong but as normal. As Carnes explains:

> Masturbation is an essential part of being a sexual person.
> Nurturing oneself, exploring sexual needs and fantasies, and
> establishing a basic self-knowledge are vital contributions
> that masturbation makes to sexual identity ... In fact, for
> people who suffer from sexual dysfunction, therapy often
> involves a careful rebuilding of a patient's attitudes and
> beliefs around masturbation.[111]

Masturbation is practiced by the majority of men and women around the world, single and married, of all races and nationalities. Biologically, there is no evidence of physical harm from periodic masturbation.

The controversy over masturbation comes from the Christian community. Although widespread and normalized by the non-Christian world, Christians wrestle over whether moderate masturbation is sinful. Christians ask, "Is masturbation acceptable to God? Is it even the will of God? Isn't masturbation God's gift to singles to keep them from fornicating until they marry? Since there are no verses in the Bible specifically addressing the issue of masturbation, isn't it left to each Christian to decide if it is right for him or her? Isn't it an issue of personal liberty for Christians?"

The issue is a moral one and the Christian community is split over it. Good and godly men and women fall on both sides of the issue. I believe that masturbation is sinful behavior and, as such, is not acceptable for the Christian who seeks to walk in sexual purity. Skarnulis quotes Willard Harley in saying, "My basic rule for marriages is that all your sex including fantasies, should be with each other. First, your wife will want it that way.

---

[111] Carnes, 2001, pp. 38, 39.

Second, if your wife is your exclusive sexual outlet, you'll have a much better romantic relationship."[112] Black writes, "pornography has a very simple goal: masturbation ... Beyond that, the goal of the pornography and the masturbation is to create a substitute for intimacy. Masturbation is sex with yourself. If I'm having sex with myself, I don't have to invest myself in another person. People who are 'addicted' to pornography aren't so much addicted to lurid material as they're addicted to self-centeredness."[113]

In the appendix of this book twelve reasons are listed for why masturbation is not God's will for anyone. Here are two overarching considerations regarding masturbation:

(a) The majority is not always right. Popularity or high percentages don't equate to the will of God. The fact that a large percentage of people are practicing masturbation doesn't make it right. Jesus said that a high percentage of human beings are on the broad road to destruction and that a small percentage will enter through the small gate to walk on the narrow way. The majority isn't always right.

(b) Biblical principles are compelling. Like many contemporary issues (marijuana, crack cocaine addiction, caffeine addiction, etc.) masturbation is not specifically mentioned in the Bible. Does an argument from silence, however, mean that God has provided no guidance and has no opinion on the issue? Hardly. Where Scripture does not mention specific contemporary issues, good hermeneutics compel Christians to turn to the

---

[112] Leanna Skarnulis, *Is Solo Sex Hurting Your Relationship?* (Retrieved January 24, 2004from http://my.webmd.com/content/Article/70/81144.htm, July 14, 2003).

[113] Jeffrey S. Black, "Pornography, Masturbation, and Other Private Misuses: A Perversion of Intimacy" (*The Journal of Biblical Counseling , 13 (3)*, 1995), p. 8.

principles given in Scripture that underlie our moral values and behaviors.

From the previous discussion on neurochemicals, masturbation causes the flow of dopamine. The release of dopamine creates a "high" for the masturbator. Because of the progressive nature of sexual addiction, increased levels of masturbation are required to achieve the same dopamine "high." Only the complete cessation of masturbation will allow dopamine levels in the brain to return to the normal range.

Finally, many therapists and researchers in the field of sexual addiction acknowledge the importance for addicts to abstain from masturbation to restore sexual health. Carnes notes:

> There is general agreement that early in recovery people should abstain from masturbation. Several factors argue for abstinence. First, masturbation involves fantasies, and the task of separating obsessive fantasies from healthy ones is too hard. Second, abstinence from masturbation helps the search for new forms of sexual expression. And, finally, for many masturbation is part of the problem and early in recovery their denial is too great for them to admit it.[114]

Emotional causes of sexual addiction.

The literature is unanimous in acknowledging that emotions play a key role in causing sexual addiction. Figure 2 illustrates how emotional responses play an important role in the sexual addiction cycle. [115]

---

[114] Carnes, *Don't Call it Love,* 1992, p. 248.
[115] Carnes, *Out of the Shadows,* 2001, p. 26.

Figure 2

Christian Sexual Addiction Cycle

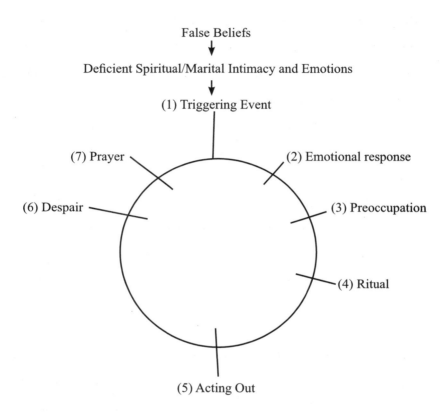

False Beliefs

Deficient Spiritual/Marital Intimacy and Emotions

(1) Triggering Event

(7) Prayer   (2) Emotional response

(6) Despair   (3) Preoccupation

(4) Ritual

(5) Acting Out

In my modification of the Carnes' Sexual Addiction Cycle, there are two pre-cycle stages, the belief stage and the deficient spiritual/marital intimacy and emotions stage. The beliefs about oneself and one's world gained from the family-of-origin, self-perception, and environment determine the level of spiritual and marital intimacy of the addict. Those beliefs also inform the emotions of the sexual addict. Emotions, such as loneliness, anger, boredom, rejection, abandonment, are then triggered by events. Those triggering events can be a spouse leaving, an argument with a boss, spouse, or children, financial stress, or unanswered prayers. The acrostic H.A.L.T. (hungry, angry, lonely, tired) is cited in the addiction literature as the classic four triggers of any addiction.[116] My experience in dealing with men in the purity ministry has led me to believe that two additional letters should be added to the H.A.L.T. acrostic: "B" for bored and "C" for curious. Boredom and curiosity are often cited by men as the reasons for acting out.

The emotional response to that triggering event leads to preoccupation in the addict. The thinking of the addict becomes consumed with lust for the sexual behavior. Preoccupation paves the way for the ritual. Rituals are the addict's plans for sexually acting out. Rituals can be as simple as logging on to the Internet on the computer or as complex as withdrawing money, flying to another city, checking into a specific hotel, contacting a lover or prostitute for sex, and returning home. Rituals are then carried out in the acting out stage. The plans are carried out and the sexual urges heeded. Because the acting out produces only a short-term euphoric high, the addict soon plunges into an emotional low. This low is despair. Addicts feel despair because they failed again, sinned again, gave in to sinful desires again. Addicts in despair verbally and mentally beat themselves up over their lack of willpower. In that state of emotional hopelessness, Christian addicts feel remorse over their sin and turn to prayer and plead with God for forgiveness and cleansing. Christian addicts feel forgiven and, with renewed resolve,

---

[116] Anonymous. *Sexaholics Anonymous* (Simi Valley, CA: SA Literature, 1989); CompCare Publishers, *Hope & Recovery: A Twelve Step Guide to Healing from Compulsive Sexual Behavior* (Minneapolis, MN: CompCare Publications, 1987).

attempt to cling to their sexual sobriety.[117]

> Sexaholics Anonymous states:
>
> When we try to use food or sex to reduce isolation,
> loneliness, insecurity, fear, tension, or to cover our
> emotions, make us feel alive, help us escape, or satisfy our
> God-hunger, we create an unnatural appetite that misuses
> and abuses the natural instinct. It is not only more intense
> than the natural but becomes something totally different.
> Eating and sex enter a different dimension; they possess an
> unnatural spiritual component.[118]

Sexual fantasy.

Sexual fantasy is one of the three building blocks of sexual addiction. Laaser calls sexual fantasy "the cornerstone for the three building blocks."[119] It is one of the major internal causes of sexual addiction. Sexual fantasy is not simply thinking about sex. Nearly everyone thinks about sex. Sexual fantasy for addicts is thinking about sex *constantly*. Whether in the form of remembering pornography viewed in the past, recollecting past sexual experiences, fantasizing about new sexual experiences in the future, or dwelling on the image of the attractive waitress at the diner, the sexual addict cannot stop fantasizing about sex. Because those mental images are always in the minds of addicts and because thinking about them triggers the release of neurochemicals to elevate their moods, sexual addicts do not need pornography to become aroused. It is possible for sexual addicts to be drug addicts, addicted to the neurochemicals secreted in their own brains.[120]

---

[117] Laaser, 2004, pp. 59-63.

[118] Anonymous, 1989, p. 41.

[119] Laaser, 2004, p. 29.

[120] Satinover, 2004; Woolf, *Purity Platoon Battle Plans* (Maple Grove, MN:

Spiritual causes of sexual addiction.

Sexual addiction is a complex, multi-causal problem. This means that it must be therapeutically addressed on multiple fronts. Secular treatment plans put the lion's share of emphasis on the physical and emotional causes of the addiction. The spiritual causes are minimally, if ever, considered.

The spiritual causes, however, are the core of the problem. There is a sexual-spiritual connection as illustrated in The Sexual-Spiritual Connection Table. It makes sense that there is a connection since both are issues of the heart. As Black notes, "Sexuality is a spiritual act, not a biological one. It's not a problem of dealing with our drives but of sanctifying our hearts."[121]

The Sexual-Spiritual Connection

	Healthy Sexual Relationship	Healthy Spiritual Relationship
Characterized by	Intimacy with spouse	Intimacy with God
Nature of relationship	Union with spouse	Union with God
Identity confirmation	Manhood/womanhood	Son/daughter of God
Core of relationship	Heart connection	Heart connection
Entry point of relationship	Marriage	New birth
Relationship effect	Healthy bond with spouse	Healthy bond with God
Relationship consequence	Increasing growth and depth	Increasing growth and depth

(continued)

National Coalition For Purity, 2008), pp. 91, 92.
[121]   Black, p. 10.

The Sexual-Spiritual Connection (continued)

	Unhealthy Sexual Relationship	Unhealthy Spiritual Relationship
Characterized by	Broken marital covenant, vows of fidelity reneged	Broken spiritual covenant, vows of fidelity reneged
Nature of relationship	Separation and distance	Separation and distance
Identity confusion	Marital identity confusion (often gender confusion)	Spiritual identity confusion (often salvation confusion)
Core of relationship	Idolatry of heart	Idolatry of heart
Entry point of relationship	Sexual adultery	Spiritual adultery
Relationship effect	Wounded partner—spouse	Wounded partner—God
Relationship consequence	Separation/divorce	Separation/discipline (slavery, sickness, death)

As described in the Introduction, sexual addiction is a sin. It is nothing less than idolatry. Addicts have choices. Though external factors such as family-of-origin, pornography, and early childhood sexualization, and internal factors such as brain chemistry, loneliness, anger, and boredom are powerful, they can be overcome. Sexual addicts are not powerless victims without choice. Though difficult, godly choices can be made, and the flesh can be silenced. Sexual addicts do it every day when they commit themselves to a recovery group.

Sexual addiction has a spiritual cause. That cause is a heart that is not in love with God and does not trust God. It is a hungry heart that seeks to meet its own needs for intimacy and love through the flesh rather than through God. When that happens, sex becomes nothing less than an idol in the heart of the addict. The addict worships that idol with every sexual thought, behavior, and word. Soon the addict is serving the idol with every breath. Soon the addict becomes like that which he or she worships. Gerald May says of addiction:

> Spiritually, addiction is a deep-seated form of idolatry. The objects of our addictions become our false gods. These are what we worship, what we attend to, where we give our time and energy, *instead of love*. Addiction, then, displaces and supplants God's love as the source and object of our deepest true desire. It is, as one modern spiritual writer has called it, a "counterfeit of religious presence."[122]

Sexual addiction disregards God's design for human sexuality. Sexual immorality is glorified and flaunted as acceptable, sophisticated, and exciting. It denigrates human beings as image bearers of God and turns them into body parts to be visually consumed by sexual cannibals.

Appendix B contains a self-test assessment for sexual addiction called, "Am I Sexually Addicted? Assessment." As with Carnes' Sexual Addiction Screening Test (SAST), the "Am I Sexually Addicted? Assessment" has shown a high discriminating ability between sexual addicts and non-addicts when the scores are above 13. All the yes-responses on the "Am I ...? " are counted. Scores of 11–12 indicate "possible 'hidden' sex addict" while scores of 13 and above indicates "probable sex addict." Like the SAST, the "Am I ...?" is not a reliable instrument for measuring sexual addiction in homosexuals, females, or adolescents.

---

[122] Gerald May, *Addiction & Grace: Love and Spirituality in the Healing of Addictions* (New York, NY: HarperCollins Publishers, 1988), p. 13.

CHAPTER SIX
THE POWER OF A PURE MAN

How can a young man keep his way pure? By living according to your word.

Psalm 119:9

I made a covenant with my eyes not to look lustfully at a girl.

Job 31:1

Men: The Key to the Family, Church, and Society

I ask, "What's wrong with the world?"

You reply, "You mean besides famine, pestilence, crime, wars, drugs, and natural disasters?"

All of those are symptoms that something deeper, more basic is wrong with the world. So, again, I ask, "What's wrong with the world?"

God's provision for a sin-sick world is the church. The church is to be the "salt" and "light of the world" (Matt. 5:13–14). If the church was functioning as the preservative in the world and as the light in the midst of the darkness like Jesus said she should, we would not be seeing the obvious symptoms of sin sickness that we see on every hand.

So then the question we need to ask is, "What's wrong with the church?" If the church is not functioning as salt and light in the world, could it be that local churches which comprise the universal church are not functioning as salt and light in their communities? After all, visible, tangible local churches of believers in Jesus Christ all around the globe form the invisible, intangible universal church of Jesus Christ. If those local churches are not salt and light, their communities are affected. This leads naturally to the question, "What's wrong with the local church?"

"Why is the local church not the salt and light she is called to be?" Could it be because the family, the primary building block of the local church, is not salt and light in the church

So, the real question is, "What's wrong with the family? Why isn't it functioning as salt and light?" I believe the answer is found in men. Men have been called by God to love, lead, sacrifice, sanctify, provide, and protect their families. To the extent that they fail to do what God has called them to do, the family suffers. It cannot be the salt and light it is called to be. If families are not salt and light, neither will their churches be. If churches are not salt and light, neither will the universal church be. If the universal church is not salt and light, the world will struggle with sin sickness and its symptoms. Men are the key. So what is a man? What makes a man a man? Is a man more than just not a woman? Is manhood different than simply being a male of the species? What makes an authentic man?

Authentic Manhood

There are biological differences between a man and a woman, but does authentic manhood go beyond the biological? Is a man defined by what he does or by who he is? One thing is certain. Men cannot take their cues for defining manhood from the culture around them. Culture is like shifting sand, constantly changing in its values. What culturally defined men in one generation, no longer defines them in the next. Manhood cannot be defined by what a man does. In a former generation, men performed work outside the home, women inside the home. Men were in business and the trades, women were homemakers. A man's identity came from his work as an accountant, a plumber, a doctor, a construction worker. That is no longer the case. The culture has shifted and work outside the home is no longer the exclusive province of men.

To discover what makes a man an authentic man, we must transcend time, race, and culture. Authentic manhood is manhood, not as prescribed by the culture in which one lives, but manhood as God designed it. The standard for manhood must be the same standard in all generations, in every culture, in every race. It is manhood according to God's design in the Bible. God has not left us to our own devices and definitions of manhood. He has given us clear teaching and a perfect model.

The Bible describes true manhood as more than being a male of the species. It is manhood as seen in the person of Jesus Christ. He is the perfect model of authentic manhood. According to the Westminster Confession of Faith, Jesus was "… very God and very man, yet one Christ, the only Mediator between God and man."[123] The Bible says, "The Word became flesh and made his dwelling among us. We have seen his glory, the glory of the One and Only, who came from the Father, full of grace and truth" (John 1:14). Since Jesus Christ is the perfect God-man, He alone is the model for authentic

---

[123] Office of the General Assembly, "The Westminster Confession of Faith," in *The Constitution of the Presbyterian Church (U.S.A.): Part 1, Book of Confessions* (New York, NY: The Office of the General Assembly, 1983), p. 6.044.

manhood. How He functioned is how authentic manhood ought to function. He truly was the "salt of the earth" and the "light of the world" (John 8:12).

Jesus Christ, God's Model of Manhood

Based upon the model of Jesus Christ, what is authentic manhood? More than what He did, Jesus' manhood was rooted in who He was. Jesus was God's Son, the Savior of the world. Jesus knew who He was. He knew He was God. He declared, "I and the Father are one" (John 10:30) and "... I am the Son of God" (John 10:36 NASV). Jesus had self-awareness. He knew His identity. Based upon His identity as the Son of God, Jesus was committed to doing His Father's will (John 5:30). He knew why He was born. He said He was a king (John 18:37) who had come to die for the sin of His people (John 12:32–33). Jesus understood that, as the Messiah, He was sent to earth to fulfill the prophecies of the Old Testament. So authentic manhood begins with knowing who you are (your identity) and why you are here (your purpose). Believers are those who are "born again" and whose identities are "in Christ." Their purpose is the same as that of Jesus Christ, to do the will of God. So what is the will of God for men?

The Six Primary Responsibilities of a Man

Roles are different than responsibilities. Roles are the parts we play in life. Responsibilities are the actions we take to carry out those roles. Jesus Christ played many roles while on earth: prophet, priest, king, suffering servant, son, brother, and Savior. So men, too, play many roles such as husband, father, son, brother, worker, friend, boss, citizen, and student. While roles may differ, if we look at Jesus' relationship to His Church in Ephesians 5:22–33 and compare that to Jesus' high priestly prayer for His Church in John 17:1–26, we find six different responsibilities He carried out which every man needs to perform regardless of his roles. These six responsibilities transcend time and culture and are universally applicable to all men. Like Jesus, every man is called to:

(a) lead (Eph. 5:23)

(b) love (Eph. 5:25)

(c) sacrifice (Eph. 5:25)

(d) sanctify (Eph. 5:26–27; John 17:17)

(e) provide (John 17:14, 22, 26; Eph. 5:29)

(f) protect (John 17:11–12, 15)

Authentic Men Have a Need to Lead

Men have been designed by God to lead. They are to be the heads of their wives and their families. Ephesians 5:23 says, "For the husband is the head of the wife as Christ is the head of the church, his body, of which he is the Savior." The word used for "head" in the New Testament is the word κεφαλὴ [*kephalē*] (English word, "cephalic") which is translated, "when used literally, head, of a man or beast; when used figuratively, to denote superior rank."[124] Wayne Grudem says, "A word's meaning is found by examining its use in various contexts. *Kephalē* is found in over fifty contexts where it refers to people who have authority over others of whom they are the "head."[125] Men have the role as the head of their wives and families. The responsibility of a head is to lovingly lead.

The relationship between Christ and the Father is the model for leadership.

What does it mean to be the head of a wife? It means that a man

---

[124] Arndt & Gingrich, p. 431.

[125] Wayne B. Grudem, *Evangelical Feminism & Biblical Truth: An Analysis of More than 100 Disputed Questions* (Sisters, OR: Multnomah Publishers, 2004), p. 202.

must lead with love. The apostle Paul writes in 1 Corinthians 11:3, "Now I want you to realize that the head of every man is Christ, and the head of the woman is man, and the head of Christ is God." In this verse, Paul lays out the "economic subordination of roles" in heaven and on earth. Just as God, the Father, is the head of Jesus Christ with no diminishing of importance, equality, respect, or significance, so a husband functions as head of his wife. Christ and the Father are equal in every respect as members of the godhead, but when it comes to the responsibilities each must fulfill, there is headship and submission. Why is God head of Christ? He is head for the sake of authority, order, and example. We are to pattern our relationships as men and women after the relationship between Christ and the Father. Headship provides order to relationships instead of confusion. God is not the God of confusion (1 Cor. 14:33 NASV).

Headship does not imply tyranny or despotism. The Bible never sanctions a husband lording it over his wife nor is the wife to usurp his role as head of the home. Rather the husband is to lead as the loving, humble head and the wife is to submit as the joyful, intelligent heart of the home.[126] God loves His Son and as His head never asks Him to do anything which is not for His benefit. The Son submits to the Father trusting His Father's love completely knowing He would never hurt Him. Both headship and submission find their model in the godhead and both are critical to family well-being.

Practicalities of headship.

Husbands are to function in their role as head of the wife just as God the Father functions in His role as Head of Jesus Christ. What does headship (leadership) look like in practical terms? Headship means loving your wife

---

[126] Ibid., p. 43

enough to only do what is in her best interest. It means expressing

Just as God, the Father, made His will clearly known to His Son (John 6:38), so a husband needs to let his wife clearly know what he thinks and what he desires. Wives ought not to have to guess what their husbands think or what their will is on an issue. Headship means prioritizing unity in leadership. Because a husband and wife are one (Eph. 5:31), it is imperative that a husband and wife be one in decision-making. Both need to be on the same page. Biblical headship is not an excuse for autonomous decision-making by a husband. A wise husband desires his wife's input before making any major decision. Wives must be encouraged to give their husbands the benefit of their counsel, insight, and wisdom. Such input allows husbands and wives to "be on the same page" and presents a unified front to the children. Finally, headship means praying and making wise decisions. Once wise counsel has been received from their wives, husbands must pray and spread the matter before the Lord. The husband must not be afraid to make a decision. Fear of making a bad decision paralyzes far too many men. Once the decision is made, a wife needs to support it for the sake of unity.

Authentic Men Are Created to Love

The second responsibility of all men is to love. In Ephesians 5:25, Paul writes, "Husbands, love your wives, just as Christ loved the church and gave himself up for her." Men have both the privilege and responsibility to love. Christ said that "by this all men will know that you are my disciples, if you love one another" (John 13:35). Love for others and especially for our wives is a mark of a godly man.

The three loves of a man.

Physical Love. The Greek word ερωζ [eros] is a physical love and gives us the English term "erotic". Lewis and Demarest call eros a "self-seeking love."[127] It is sensual and sexual in nature. A husband must love his wife erotically. Erotic love involves physical touching (massages, hand holding, back scratches, kissing, touching, etc.). Erotic love involves the body thus hygiene and cleanliness must be a high priority. For women, sexual intimacy flows out of emotional intimacy which flows out of trust which flows out of honest communication which flows out of time together as described in Diagram A.

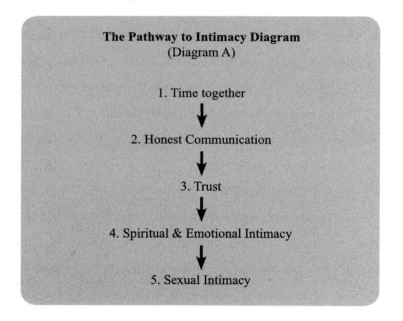

The Pathway to Intimacy Diagram
(Diagram A)

1. Time together
↓
2. Honest Communication
↓
3. Trust
↓
4. Spiritual & Emotional Intimacy
↓
5. Sexual Intimacy

One writer has said that when it comes to sex, "men are like

---

[127] Lewis & Demarest, *Integrative Theology,* vol. 1, p. 235.

microwaves and women are like crock pots."[128] What she means is that men become aroused quickly and are done quickly. Men want to move from stage one to stage five skipping stages two through four in Diagram A. Women on the other hand are like crock pots in that they heat up slowly and stay hot for a longer period of time. Women typically need to go through all five stages to become sexually intimate. Unlike men, who require little foreplay to become sexually aroused, sexual arousal for women involves slow, lengthy foreplay. Erotic love also means appealing to all five senses: touching, tasting, hearing, seeing, smelling. Erotic love means splashing on cologne, giving flowers, practicing good table etiquette, speaking kindly, etc. The world's advertising lives by the adage, "sex sells." Eros is a driving force behind much of the world's economy.

2. Soul Love. The second way we are to love our wives is with φιλία [*philia*] love. Philia love corresponds to emotional or soul love. It is the bond of love found between good friends giving us the English word *Philadelphia*, "city of brotherly love." To love our wives with philia love is to love them emotionally and to bond to them with our emotions. Emotional bonding or intimacy takes place as we move through stages one through three in Diagram A. Wives require their husband's time and honesty to begin to trust them. Once trust has been earned, emotional bonds of attachment can begin to be built. Emotional love knits our souls together with our wives. It makes the "two into one." Philia love is reflected in the heart longing of a husband to be with his wife when they are apart, the joy and delight he feels in her presence, and the desire he has to please and protect her. Philia is the love the world

---

[128] Lauren Bull, *American Youth Uninformed on Sexual Health* (Retrieved July 7, 2008 from RH Reality Check: http://www.rhrealitycheck.org/ blog/2007/11/01/american-youth-seriously-uninformed-on-sexual-health, November 1, 2007).

pursues with all its might. Soul love uses an "in" language only understood by the couple. They call each other by pet names reflecting the intimacy of their relationship. Soul love prompts love letters, spontaneous phone calls, and gifts.

3. Spiritual Love. The third way we are to love our wives is spiritually with ἀγαπή [*agapē*] love.[129] Agapē love is the love of God produced in Christians by the indwelling Holy Spirit (Gal. 5:22). Because agapē love is supernatural in origin and comes from God alone, it cannot be produced by the flesh. Only the Holy Spirit can give us the power to love our wives with agapē love (Eph. 5:18). This is the type of love Jesus Christ has for His Bride, the church. A Godly husband loves his wife just as Christ loves the church. He loves her with a three-way love: physically, soulishly, and spiritually.

Authentic Men Are To Sacrifice Like Christ

Christ came to be the Lamb of God, the Sacrifice for the sin of the world. As mentioned on a previous page, love always involves sacrifice. Sacrifice means "to slaughter or kill, often used in connection with an altar."[130] Men are called to sacrifice even as Christ "did not come to be served, but to serve, and to give His life as a ransom for many" (Matt. 20:28). Ephesians 5:25 says, "Husbands, love your wives, just as Christ loved the church and gave himself up for her." Even so, husbands are to give themselves up for

---

[129]   Lewis and Demarest explain the distinction between φιλία [philia] and ἀγάπη [agapē] when they write: *Phileō* denotes affection, concern, and fondness resulting from a *personal relationship*, and in this sense it is used of God's love for the Son (John 5:20) and for Christian believers (John 16:27). *Agapaō/Agape* connotes affection or deep regard resulting from a *deliberate choice*, and so is used of God's love for Christ (John 3:35; 1:17; 15:9; 17:24, 26), Christian believers (John 17:23; 1 John 3:1; 4:19), and the entire human race (John 3:16). Lewis & Demarest, 1:350, 352 (italics added).

[130]   Θύω, Arndt & Gingrich, p. 367.

their wives. Agapē love drives a man to willingly lay down his life for the sake of his bride.

The face of sacrifice.

What does sacrifice look like for a man who strives to be authentic? The nature of sacrifice is to die, give up, do without, pay a price. Whether it is giving up presumed rights and accepting the responsibilities of adulthood, the authentic man will practice a life of sacrifice. What will that kind of life look like? For the godly man it will take the form of sacrificing time, talent, treasure, and selfishness.

The most valuable commodity we possess is time. We steward time. It does not belong to us. God knows the number of days allotted to each of us. The man who wants to be like Christ will sacrifice his time to be with his wife. He will prioritize her above all other relationships in his life. As Cloud and Townsend say, "… in order to say yes to keeping a close marriage, you will have to say no to lots of other things. A life of 'yes' to everything else ultimately results in a 'no' to your marriage."[131]

It will mean sacrificing talent. God has gifted every man with natural talents and spiritual gifts. The authentic man will use his natural talents to benefit his wife and children. Unlike the cobbler whose family had holes in their shoes, a man who sacrifices his talent will put his wife's projects first on his "to do" list. He will teach the skills he has learned to his children.

He must sacrifice his treasure. Mammon cannot be permitted to be his master (Matt. 6:24 NASV). Mammon is the wealth this world treasures: money and the possessions it buys. We must choose whom we treasure— Christ or mammon. Authentic men treasure Christ.

---

[131] Cloud & Townsend, *Boundaries in Marriage,* p. 149.

He will sacrifice his selfishness. The Bible says that men are good at caring for their own needs (Eph. 5:29). Selfishness comes naturally to the human heart. The psalmist pleads, "Turn my heart toward your statutes and not toward selfish gain" (Ps. 119:36). As mentioned, authentic men readily lay down their presumed rights and pick up their responsibilities. They are "presumed rights" because we have died with Christ and all our rights died with us. Now the life we live is by faith in the Son of God (Gal. 2:20).

Authentic Men Are to Sanctify Themselves and Others

The fourth responsibility of an authentic man is to sanctify others, especially his wife and children. To sanctify someone is to set them apart for holy purposes. Just as the priests of the Old Testament were set apart for the holy purpose of serving the Lord, so authentic men sanctify themselves, their wives, and others. Ephesians 5:25–27 says:

Husbands, love your wives, just as Christ loved the church

and gave himself up for her to make her holy, cleansing her

by the washing with water through the word, and to present

her to himself as a radiant church, without stain or wrinkle

or any other blemish, but holy and blameless.

So the command for husbands to love their wives is linked to both sacrifice and sanctification. When a husband loves his wife, he will sacrifice himself for her to make her holy. He will spiritually wash her with the water of the Word of God, teaching her purity. Jesus confirms that when He asks the Father to, "Sanctify them [His followers] by the truth; your word is truth" (John 17:17). Jesus is asking the Father to set His followers apart for holy purposes by using the truth of the Word of God to purify them. The Bible is God's instrument for purifying others. The psalmist declares, "How can a young man keep his way pure? By living according to your word" (Ps. 119:9).

Practicalities of sanctifying others.

The authentic man will first sanctify his own life by obeying the Word. He will purify his speech, conduct, and attitudes. He will cleanse his life from deceitful speech (1 Pet. 3:10) by speaking truth to others and refusing to lie or manipulate the truth. He will teach others the same. He will cleanse his life from obscenity and filthy speech (Eph. 5:4). He will set the example for others by asking the Lord to "set a guard over my mouth, O LORD; keep watch over the door of my lips" (Ps. 141:3). He will teach his wife and children to be truth-tellers who refuse to lie, regardless of the consequences. He will sing praises to the Lord and give Him thanks with all his heart for all things (Eph. 5:19).

He will sanctify his wife (Eph. 5:26). Agapē love cleanses and makes the bride holy. Agapē love causes a man to pray with and for his bride; to teach her the Word of God; to lead her in practicing sexual purity, guarding what they view for entertainment; to practice modesty with her and his children, guarding what they say and do in front of the children.

He will conduct himself "in a manner worthy of the gospel of Christ" (Phil. 1:27). He will flee evil of all kinds including stealing, sexual immorality, idolatry, and the love of money (1 Cor. 6:18, 10:14; Eph. 4:28; 1 Tim. 6:11). He will treasure Christ above all, knowing that He is the antidote to idolatry. He will model this value for others and teach it to his wife and children. He will keep a clear conscience so he might silence his critics.

The authentic man bent on sanctifying himself and others will guard his heart for "it is the wellspring of life" (Prov. 4:23). He will shun ungodly attitudes of bitterness, rage, anger, hatred, greed, selfishness, and unbelief, all of which defile a man's heart (Eph. 4:31; Col. 3:5; Heb. 3:12). Whatever fills a man's heart comes out of his mouth (Matt. 15:18). Ungodly attitudes of the heart are heard in his speech. He teaches his wife and children that attitudes are just as capable of being sinful as speech and behavior.

Authentic Men Provide for Their Wives and Children

This was the primary role (some would say the only role) husbands in previous generations played. As the sole "breadwinner" for the family, husbands in previous eras were first and foremost providers who worked hard and brought home "the bacon." In today's culture, many families depend upon two incomes and husbands are often not the sole provider. As we shall see, the provider role of the husband is still a valid and necessary role. Providing for his own is instinctively written in the hearts of every man. Few things are as devastating to a man as the loss of his job. For many men, to lose their jobs is to lose their identity and meaning in life. So providing is a deeply-ingrained value in the heart of an authentic man. Jesus affirmed this value when He prayed:

> I pray for them. I am not praying for the world, but for those
> you have given me, for they are yours… I have given them
> your word and the world has hated them, for they are not of
> the world any more than I am of the world… I have given
> them the glory that you gave me, that they may be one as
> we are one… I have made you known to them, and will
> continue to make you known in order that the love you have
> for me may be in them and that I myself may be in them
> (John 17:9, 14, 22, 26).

Jesus provided well for His disciples and others. Besides the material provisions of turning water into wine (John 2:1–11) and feeding 5,000 on one occasion and 4,000 on another (Matt 16:9–10), Jesus provided His disciples with the spiritual provisions of prayer, the word, His Father's glory, and knowledge of His Father (John 17:9, 14, 22, 26).

How does a man provide?

An authentic man provides in four ways: physically, emotionally, spiritually, and relationally.

He provides through physical provision. When the Bible speaks of a husband providing for his family, it speaks of him providing the basic necessities of life: food, clothing, shelter. At the bare minimum, a husband must provide his wife with food on the table, clothes on her back, and a roof over her head. In 1 Timothy 6:8, Paul says, "But if we have food and clothing, we will be content with that." James writes, "Suppose a brother or sister is without clothes and daily food" (James 2:15). The Bible exhorts men not to be lazy or sluggards but to work hard and provide for their families. Does this mean that a wife cannot work or help with the financial provision of the family? No. Proverbs 31:16, 24 says that a virtuous wife, "considers a field and buys it; out of her earning she plants a vineyard … She makes linen garments and sells them, and supplies the merchants with sashes." This wife is both entrepreneurial and ambitious. She contributes to the family finances. Although she can help, the husband should be the chief supplier of physical resources. He is the one to whom God gave the responsibility and privilege of providing for the family.

Secondly, he provides through emotional provision. How does a husband provide for his wife emotionally? Just as he provides for her physical needs, so he provides for her emotional needs. What emotional needs do wives have? Wives need to feel loved, heard, protected, wanted, safe, beautiful, and valued. A wise husband will provide all seven critical emotional needs for his wife. How can he do that? He can do that by verbally telling her she is beautiful and valuable and by physically touching her and wanting her. He can do that by serving her with his talents and by sacrificing his time for her. He can do that by caring more about her needs that his own and by listening to her when she speaks and not disrespecting her opinion. He can do that by spending more money on her than he should and by standing up for her when others are attacking her. He can do that by treating her as his sister-in-Christ, not simply as his wife.

The godly man provides for his wife and children through spiritual provision. An authentic husband provides for his wife physically and emotionally, but the most important type of provision he can provide is spiritual provision. The Bible says, "What good is it for a man to gain the whole world, yet forfeit his soul?" (Mark 8:36). In the same way, what good does it do for a husband to only provide for his wife physically and emotionally? If she is an unbeliever, she will be separated from him for eternity. Spiritual provision is the most important provision of all! How can a husband spiritually provide for his wife? By sharing the Gospel of Jesus Christ with her and gently encouraging her to receive Christ Jesus as her Savior if she does not yet know Him. Paul recognizes that not all wives and husbands will believe when he writes, "How do you know, wife, whether you will save your husband? Or, how do you know, husband, whether you will save your wife?" (1 Cor. 7:16). The answer is you don't know but that doesn't mean a believing husband should not pray for his unbelieving wife and share Christ with her. If a husband has a believing wife, spiritual provision takes the form of encouraging her in her spiritual growth. The godly husband does this by praying for her and with her, teaching her the Bible through couple devotions, prioritizing corporate worship with her, establishing the tithe as their standard for financial giving, and paying for her to attend spiritual growth opportunities (retreats, seminars, conferences, etc.).

It is vitally important for a man to lead in spiritual things. He leads his wife and children in worship. He leads them in both public worship in church and private worship through personal and family devotions. He leads them to take communion together and be baptized.

As the family priest, husbands must pray with their wives and children at meals and at bedtime. Prayer with one's wife is bonding and unifying. It helps a man to be "on the same page" with his wife. Prioritize praying together at bedtime. This will mean going to sleep in the same bed, going to bed at the same time, praying together before going to sleep, praying for each other and your children, praying for the protection of Christ's blood against anything demonic interfering with your sleep, and praying for sound sleep and sweet dreams. Pray and fast together as husband and wife when facing weighty decisions.

Finally, husbands must pray for and lead their children to personally receive Jesus Christ as Savior and Lord. The husband is the key to the whole family becoming believers. Consider the story of the Philippian jailer and his family recorded in Acts 16:30–34:

> He then brought them out and asked, "Sirs, what must I do to be saved?"
>
> They replied, "Believe in the Lord Jesus, and you will be saved—you and your household." Then they spoke the word of the Lord to him

and to all the others in his house. At that hour of the night the jailer took them and washed their wounds; then immediately he and all his family were baptized. The jailer brought them into his house and set a meal before them; he was filled with joy because he had come to believe in God—he and his whole family.

God's desire is for whole families to receive Jesus Christ and be saved! Husbands are the keys to that happening.

Finally, husbands are to make relational provision for their wives and children. Women are highly relational people. Psychologists call wives the "relationship-minders" of the family. They are concerned that everyone in the family is getting along well and that family relationships are strong and functioning. They get concerned when those relationships are out of whack. Because they are relationally minded, a godly husband will provide relationally for his wife. He will encourage her to spend time with her female friends, with her children, and with her parents. These relationships are important to her. A wise husband recognizes that fact and makes provision for her to cultivate appropriate relationships.

An authentic man functions as the provider for his own. He provides for his wife and children. He provides his wife with more than the physical necessities of life. He provides for her emotionally, spiritually, and relationally as well. He knows that by caring for his wife, he is really caring for himself for, "He who loves his wife loves himself. After all, no one ever hated his own body, but he feeds and cares for it, just as Christ does the church" (Eph. 5:28–29).

Authentic Men Protect Those With Whom They Have Been Entrusted

Most men need to be taught to protect others. It is safe to say that most men are more inclined to be self-protective than other-protective. Why does a husband have to protect his wife? Isn't she an adult and can't she take care of herself? Yes, a wife is an adult and she may be capable of taking care of herself, but that doesn't diminish the responsibility God places on a husband to protect her. As her "head" and her leader, the overall responsibility for her protection falls to her husband. She is under his umbrella. She belongs to him and he belongs to her (Eph. 5:28). In addition, his love for her demands that he protect her and look out for her best interests. Love protects (1 Cor. 13:7). Love looks out for the interests of others (Phil. 2:4).

What is involved in protecting a wife?

The Bible uses the term "covering" to define protection. Husbands are to be the "covering" for their wives, protecting them from the storms of life. Just as God protected Israel during her wilderness wanderings, covering her with a cloud by day and a pillar of fire by night, so husbands are to cover their wives. The Hebrew verb for protect means "to cover, hide, protect" and the noun means "covering or hiding-place."[132] The psalmist writes, "Keep me as the apple of your eye; hide me in the shadow of your wings from the wicked who assail me, from my mortal enemies who surround me (Ps. 17:8–9).

How will he protect her? Husbands must protect their wives physically. As previously stated, an authentic husband physically protects his wife from anyone or anything that might harm her: bullies, parents, in-laws, relatives, neighbors, her boss, even the children. He cannot passively stand by and watch his wife being abused. He must come to her aid. He cannot permit his children or anyone else to slap, punch, shove, or in any way physically

---

[132] סָתַר [sathar], Brown, Driver, & Briggs, p. 711, 712.

abuse his wife. Under Old Testament law, children were executed for striking a parent (Exod. 21:15). Likewise, such behavior cannot be permitted today. An authentic husband must protect his wife and children. He must courageously face down all who would physically or verbally abuse them. Just as Secret Service agents who protect the president of the United States are trained to "take a bullet" for him, so husbands must willingly "take a bullet" for their wives and children should the occasion arise. Husbands must willingly sacrifice themselves for their families to protect them and keep them safe.

A husband must provide emotional protection for his wife. The authentic husband cannot permit his children or anyone else to verbally abuse his wife through ridicule, mockery, cursing, or name-calling. Again, under Old Testament law such abuse by children was considered a capital crime worthy of death (Exod. 21:17). The husband must intervene. He must defend her honor to others and stand up for her when she is being attacked.

Emotional protection will involve learning to live with your wife considerately. Peter writes to husbands, "Husbands, in the same way be considerate as you live with your wives, and treat them with respect as the weaker partner and as heirs with you of the gracious gift of life, so that nothing will hinder your prayers" (1 Pet. 3:7). The compassionate husband will seek to understand his wife. He will intentionally avoid "triggering" her emotionally by inciting her fears, her past failures, and her insecurities. He will remember that she is physically weaker than him. He will be aware of her menstrual cycle and the impact it has on her emotions. The wise husband will avoid confrontations during his wife's menstrual period.

A husband will also give spiritual protection to his wife. One of the roles a husband plays is that of the spiritual priest of his family. He stands guard over the family through his prayers. By praying for God to apply the blood of Christ to his family, the authentic husband can protect his family from demonic attack. Revelation 12:11 says, "They overcame him (Satan) by the blood of the Lamb and by the word of their testimony; they did not love their lives so much as to shrink from death." The spiritual weapons which a godly husband has at his disposal are prayer, the Bible, and the blood of Christ. He must become an expert in the use of all three weapons as the spiritual priest for his family.

The godly husband must also guard his family against false teachers, Satan's emissaries, who seek to "worm their way into homes and gain control over weak-willed women, who are loaded down with sins and are swayed by all kinds of evil desires, always learning but never able to acknowledge the truth" (2 Tim. 3:6–7). The godly husband must know what his wife and children are reading, watching, and hearing for spiritual growth. He must scrutinize all teaching to insure that it squares with the Word of God. If he is unsure whether a teaching or teacher is of God, he should seek the counsel of his pastor. If it proves to be false teaching, he must intervene to protect his own.

A godly husband protects his wife. He protects her physically, emotionally, and spiritually. He knows that in so doing he is protecting himself, for the two have become one in God's eyes.

How Does a Man Become Pure?

A man becomes pure inwardly in his heart and outwardly in his behaviors. Both are required to live in purity. To separate them is to live a false life. A man's outward life reflects that which is in his heart (Matt. 15:8). It is not possible to be pure in heart and continue in outward sexual sin.

Inward Purity

Inwardly, a man becomes pure through repentance, confession of sin, and the power of the Holy Spirit.

Repentance of sin.

Purity starts with repentance of sexual sins. Repentance means "a change of mind, turning about, conversion."[133] Repentance always results in action. Probably the best example of repentance and the action steps required is found in the story of the prodigal son in Luke 15. In that story, the son illustrates the seven basic evidences of repentance.

> "When he came to his senses, he said, 'How many of
> my father's hired men have food to spare, and here I am
> starving to death! I will set out and go back to my father and
> say to him: Father, I have sinned against heaven and against
> you. I am no longer worthy to be called your son; make me
> like one of your hired men.' So he got up and went to his
> father.
>
> "But while he was still a long way off, his father saw him
> and was filled with compassion for him; he ran to his son,
> threw his arms around him and kissed him.
>
> "The son said to him, 'Father, I have sinned against heaven
> and against you. I am no longer worthy to be called your
> son' "(Luke 15:17–21).

Repentance involves:

(a) Coming to your senses and telling yourself the truth—Luke 15:17. It means recognizing your situation, admitting your bondage, and telling

---

[133] μετάνοια [*metanoia*], Arndt & Gingrich, p. 513.

yourself the truth with no more minimizing, denying, or excuses.

(b) Recognizing what you've lost—Luke 15:17. "hired men have food to spare"

(c) Honestly assessing your current situation—Luke 15:17. "I am starving to death!"

(d) Hearing yourself commit to the action required—Luke 15:18. "I will set out and go."

(e) Seeking the forgiveness of the offended—Luke 15:18. "Father, I have sinned against heaven and against you."

(f) Doing repentant self-talk including rehearsing what you need to say— Luke 15:18–19.

(g) Being courageous and following through to do it—Luke 15:20–21. "So he got up and went to his father."

Inward purity starts with repenting over sexual sin to gain a clean heart. A pure man is humble and broken over his sin. Schaumberg writes:

> The ministry of healing requires an emphasis on repentance at the deepest levels of the heart. Because false intimacy is predictable and efficient in controlling relational pain, it becomes so powerful that the insanity of the sex addict's behavior can go far beyond his or her awareness. Trapped in the use of such power and control, a sex addict naturally does not experience the 'godly sorrow' that is necessary for repentance and true internal and external change (see 2 Cor. 7:9–11).[134]

Confession to those wounded.

Confession means to "say the same thing" as God says concerning

---

[134] Schaumberg, *False Intimacy*, pp. 196, 212, 213.

my sin; namely, that I did it.[135] Confession is humbly admitting my sins and agreeing with God concerning my guiltiness. Confession always follows and is a normal response to genuine repentance. Both repentance and confession are rooted in a humble heart. Confession requires the repentant man to apologize and ask for forgiveness for his sins from God and those he's hurt, such as his spouse, children, fiancé, girlfriend, and others. Confession requires him to echo words similar to those of the prodigal son, "I have sinned against heaven and against you" (Luke 15:18).

An authentic man who is repentant wants a genuine, no-secrets relationship with his wife, fiancé, or girlfriend. How much of his sexual sin should a man confess? Wisdom and kindness dictate that a man's desire to confess his sins must bow before the amount of information his wife, fiancée, or girlfriend desires to know. His need to tell his "stuff" is secondary to her need to know his "stuff." She may want to know only his sexual sins since the time they met, or since their wedding, or in the past year. She may want to know his entire sexual history, sometimes called a "garbage dump." For a man to arbitrarily decide to do a garbage dump on his wife without her asking for such disclosure is cruel and abusive. The amount of information and the timing of the sharing of that information should be the call of the wife, fiancée, or girlfriend—not the man. He can ask her what her needs are in this area and then confess to her all that is within her ability to handle.

The power of the Holy Spirit.

Only the Holy Spirit has the power to permanently change a heart. Only He can convict of sin, righteousness, and judgment to come (John 16:8). The Holy Spirit can turn a heart of stone into a heart of flesh, bringing new life

---

[135] Ὁμολογέω [*homologeō*] lit. "to speak the same", Arndt & Gingrich, p. 571.

to that which was dead in trespasses and sins (Ezek. 36:26; Eph. 2:1). Apart from the Holy Spirit there is only the manipulation of the flesh and no matter how skillfully we manipulate the flesh, we can never produce deep, permanent change of heart.

Outward Purity

Outward purity is purity in behavior, thought, and attitude which is seen and heard by others. Purity of the heart is seen in outward change. Three factors contribute to producing this observable purity:

Motivation—we need to be motivated to want to change. There are three types of motivation—self-motivation, love, and pain. Self-motivation is the attempt to "pull yourself up by your own bootstraps." It is trying harder. It is the self-willed inner motivation seen in the world. Self-motivation works for a while to produce surface level, external purity but it rarely lasts. Love is a powerful motivator. For love of a good woman, a man will do many things. However, the pull of sexual immorality is so powerful that, though he loves his wife and repeatedly promises her that he will quit, a man will invariably lapse back into sexual sin. Sadly, love is not enough of a motivation to produce permanent change. Finally, negative as it is, pain is the most powerful motivator known to man. Humans are pain-avoidant. Pain will drive a man or woman to change in order to make the pain stop. Emotional pain is even more effective at producing change than physical pain. The pain of a broken relationship, a failed marriage, financial bankruptcy, and fear of loss or abandonment are powerful motivators to make necessary changes.

Power—we need the power to change. We can be highly motivated but without the power to change we will be stuck with the status quo. There are two sources of power for change—the flesh and the Holy Spirit. The flesh is the power source for self-motivation. It is weak and can only provide surface changes that rarely last. The Holy Spirit is the power of God. As mentioned above, He is the only change agent who can change a heart. He has the power to purify the impure.

Knowledge—we can be motivated and have power for change but unless we know what to do and how to do it, we will likely lapse back into sexual sin. The temptation and pull of sexual sin is strong and the flesh is weak (Rom. 7:21–23). The Holy Spirit must help us to discipline our lives so that we might "share in his holiness" (Heb. 12:10–11). We need a strategy, a plan of discipline that will equip us to know what to do and how to do it. That is the purpose of a purity ministry.

> **"All three — motivation, power, and knowledge — combine to produce visible change. The purity within is now seen by the watching world."**

All three—motivation, power, and knowledge—combine to produce visible change. The purity within is now seen by the watching world.

Profile of a Pure Man

You will know a man has become pure when he has found Christ to be his treasure and his heart is captivated with Christ. He will be easily recognizable, for he has chosen to purify himself of all that defiles by setting boundaries around his speech, conduct, and attitudes. He has destroyed all pornography and cleansed the hard drive in his computer of anything ungodly or unclean. He has humbled himself and made himself accountable to a band of brothers. He captures every thought and brings it into obedience to Christ

(2 Cor. 10:5). How does he capture thoughts? One way this can be done is through visualization of Christ on the Cross. The pure man has ingrained in his mind the image of Jesus Christ hanging on the cross, blood flowing from His pierced side. He visualizes himself kneeling at the foot of the cross and feeling the blood of Christ hitting him on his head, cleansing his every thought. This becomes the default thought he uses whenever he recognizes ungodly thoughts crossing his mind.

He has made a covenant with his eyes (Job 31:1) and no longer visually snacks on the beauty of women. As part of that covenant he has learned to bounce his eyes rather than stare at a woman, starve his eyes by looking away from women who are clothed immodestly, and look at women from the "neck up" choosing to focus on their faces rather than their bodies. When out at a restaurant with his wife, fiancé, or girlfriend, he sits directly opposite her so he can look upon her beauty and avoid "alternative monitoring."[136] He does not use sexual humor. He does not dress immodestly. He chooses entertainment carefully, knowing that entertainment can be the "devil's playground." He avoids anything defiling and stands with King David in pledging, "I will set before my eyes no vile thing" (Ps. 101:3). He has ceased from masturbation (self sex) and has chosen to direct all his sexual energy toward his wife. If he's single, he practices self-control that he might not "burn" with lust (1 Cor. 7:9).

The Cost to Becoming a Pure Man

Jesus always encouraged His followers to count the cost before beginning any project (Luke 14:27–33). So must we. What will it cost a man

---

[136] "Alternative monitoring," is what a man does when he scans the horizon looking for options to the woman he is with. He is not a "one woman" man in his heart (cf. 1 Tim. 3:2, Titus 1:6).

to become pure? The ten most common costs to a man who desires to become pure are:

(a) His sexual sin. If a man has been practicing a particular sexual sin for a long period of time, to stop is like losing an old friend. Because cessation produces a vacuum, a man must fill the vacuum with righteous practices such as time in the Word of God and prayer.

(b) His rebel heart. He will need to give up his rebelliousness to authority, beginning with his rebellion against God's authority. The rebel fancies himself to be god and in charge of his own life. He must be dethroned to become pure. He must become a man under authority who humbly submits to the Lord Jesus Christ (cf. Luke 7:6–8).

(c) His isolation. The sexual sinner, because of the shame and secrecy of his sin, isolates and hides himself from relationships. To become pure he will have to sacrifice his isolationism and enter into relationships with other men and his wife (if married).

(d) His lack of intimate relationships. Elsie Woolf and Debra Laaser call sexual addiction "an intimacy disorder."[137] The man who desires to become pure will have to pay the price of entering into intimacy with his wife, fiancé, or girlfriend. He can no longer settle for shallow superficial relationships. Intimacy does not simply mean sexual intimacy. Intimacy is broader in scope than sexuality. God has said, "It is not good for the man to be alone" (Gen. 2:18). The antidote to aloneness is intimacy. Intimacy involves becoming transparent enough for a wife, fiancé, or girlfriend to "into-me-see."

(e) His impure thought life and fantasies. The ungodly man has no boundaries around his thoughts or fantasies. He is "like a city whose walls are

---

[137] Debra Laaser, personal communication, July 11, 2005; Elsie Woolf, personal communication, July 22, 2005

broken down is a man who lacks self-control" (Prov. 25:28). Without mental boundaries, Satan is able to put any thought into his mind and the man without self-control accepts it, makes it his own, and dwells on it. The pure man must take every thought captive in obedience to Christ (2 Cor. 10:5).

(f) His alternative monitoring. The pure man must become a "one woman man" (1 Tim. 3:2, Titus 1:6).[138] As a married man or a man in a committed relationship, he must pay the price of commitment to one woman. He belongs to one woman and her to him.

(g) His lack of honesty. The man who would be pure must pay the price of his lack of honesty. Men lie primarily because of fear. Because they are self-protective, they fear the consequences of the truth. To become pure, a man must begin to trust others and God enough to speak the truth. He must be forthright with his words. His "yes" must be yes and his "no," no (James 5:12). He can no longer shade the truth because half-truths are whole lies.

(h) His lack of trust. Because they are afraid of being hurt, rejected, or abandoned, men have a difficult time trusting anyone including wives, other men, or even God. To become pure, a man must learn to trust others. Trust is typically cultivated in the context of a small band of brothers who practice honesty, confidentiality, and accountability with one another. It takes time for men to learn to trust. Trust must be earned over a period of time.

(i) His lack of accountability. Most men live rather unaccountable lives. No one "holds their feet to the fire" for their choices. Men who desire purity must submit themselves to the discipline of accountability. They must permit others to speak into their lives and gently confront them on their choices.

(j) His selfishness. Finally, for a man to become pure, he must give up his

---

[138] μιᾶσ γυναικὸσ ἄνδρα [mias gunaikos andra] lit. a "one woman man." This is a man who is committed to one woman and faithful to her alone.

inherent selfishness. Born as sinners, all of us are naturally selfish demanding that our needs be met. The natural man finds it easy to be selfish. Other-awareness is not natural and must be learned.

Appendix C is a worksheet to help the reader think through the high cost of impurity. Too many think that sexual immorality and pornography, in particular, are victimless crimes that only hurt the user. That view is short-sighted and does not take into account the many areas of a person's life affected by those sins or the impact of his sin on others.

The Benefits of Living a Pure Life

Finally, what are the benefits for the man who chooses to live in purity? Here are ten of the most common benefits of living in sexual purity:

(a) A right relationship with God because he has dethroned the idol of sexual immorality in his life.

(b) Personal integrity because he has stopped living in hypocrisy. He is no longer living a double life.

(c) Spiritual freedom from bondage to sexual sin.

(d) True intimacy with his wife and the start of an authentic marriage.

(e) A fitting model as a father for his children.

(f) The ability of worship, prayer, and service with sincerity of heart.

(g) A model of true Christian manhood for other men and women.

(h) A participant in a counter-cultural revolution. By taking a stand against a common enemy, sexual immorality, he is exposing to the light the disgraceful things done in secret (Eph. 5:12–13).

(i) Victory over the enemy of his soul and taken back ground in his life that had been given over to Satan.

(j) A participant in preparing the church, the Bride of Christ, for the return of Christ and the marriage supper of the Lamb.

Is it worth it? On a cost-benefit scale, are the benefits of purity worth the cost to obtain it? The answer depends on whether a man desires to raise the bar in his life. If he's content with the status quo, he won't desire purity. He considers his life "good enough" for him. He does not want to grow closer to God or his spouse. If he did, that would mean changing—something he is fearful of doing. If, however, a man is convicted that his sin is abhorrent to God and a betrayal of his wife, he will desire purity. He will do whatever it takes to become a pure man and when he does, all the benefits listed will be his. He will find that the cost of purity is miniscule compared to the benefits.

CHAPTER SEVEN
THE POWER OF A PURE WOMAN
With Elsie E. Woolf

Charm is deceptive, and beauty is fleeting; but a woman who fears the LORD is

to be praised.

Proverbs 31:30

As a man there is only so much I can write about the power of a pure woman. It truly takes a woman to write about the power of a pure woman. I am grateful to my wife, Elsie, a model of a pure woman, for her willingness to co-author this chapter with me.

Authentic Womanhood

As was asked under the chapter on the power of a pure man, what makes a woman a woman? Is womanhood simply biological? Is a woman different than a female of the species? Is a woman the "fairer, gentler sex?" Is womanhood defined by cultural roles? Is she defined by her role in society? Although many women choose the roles of mother and homemaker, many others choose to be soldiers, businesswomen, and entrepreneurs. Since the onslaught of the feminist movement in the last quarter of the twentieth century, women have protested, voted, and demanded equal rights especially in the workplace. Through the Equal Rights Amendment and many legal decisions, women have, for the most part, achieved workplace parity with men.

If womanhood can no longer be defined by roles, what does define it? My contention is that authentic womanhood, like authentic manhood, must transcend culture, race, and time. It must be true womanhood regardless of the era or civilization. That drives us to the Bible as the sourcebook and authority for authentic womanhood. The Bible provides authoritative standards that transcend time and culture. It is prescriptive for how life is to be lived and what makes a woman authentic. The authentic woman is a biblical woman. She is defined by the standards of the Bible. So what does the Bible say about womanhood and what are the characteristics of an authentic woman?

The Primary Roles and Responsibilities of an Authentic Woman

To learn what the Bible has to say about authentic womanhood, we must turn to the place where womanhood begins, the book of Genesis. In Genesis 2:18, we find the first reason God created woman, "The LORD God said, 'It is not good for the man to be alone. I will make a helper suitable for him.' " The literal Hebrew translation of Genesis 2:18 is "And the Lord God said, 'it is not good the man being alone; I will make for him a helper corresponding to him.' " This is the first time in creation that God has declared anything "not good." Until this point, everything created by God in the first six days of creation has been declared "good" or "very good." What are the four responsibilities of an authentic woman? She is to be an intimate companion, a conspicuous complement, a mother, and a joyful submitter to her husband. Let's look at each one.

Eve was Adam's companion.

Two words catch our eye as we read Genesis 2:18: "alone" and "helper." What do they mean? The Hebrew word for alone means, "isolated, separated, alone, by oneself."[139] As a good physician, God first examines the patient and identifies the problem. What is it that is not good? It is not good for the man to be alone with no one with whom to fellowship. He needs someone corresponding to himself to take away his aloneness. The first role of a woman, even preceding the role of helper, is that of companion, one who would take away man's aloneness. God knew that man needed a companion corresponding to himself. After parading all the animals past Adam to see if any might fit the bill as a companion for him, God formed a companion for Adam from Adam himself. She would be the antidote to his aloneness. Derek Kidner writes these profound words:

> The naming of the animals, a scene which portrays man
> as monarch of all he surveys, poignantly reveals him as a
> social being, made for fellowship, not power; he will not
> live until he loves, giving himself away (2:24) to another
> on his own level. So the woman is presented wholly as
> his partner and counterpart; nothing is yet said of her as
> childbearer. She is valued for herself alone.[140]

Eve was created by God as the antidote to Adam's aloneness. Why was Adam's aloneness important to rectify? Aloneness is the opposite of intimacy. God created man to enjoy an intimate relationship with Himself and

---

[139] לְבַדּוֹ [*lebadō*] from בָּדַד [*badad*], Brown, Driver, & Briggs, p. 94.
[140] Derek Kidner, *Genesis: An Introduction and Commentary* In D. J. Wiseman (Ed.), The Tyndale Old Testament Commentaries, (Downers Grove, IL: Inter-Varsity Press, 1972), p. 65.

others, the same kind of intimacy enjoyed by the trinity within the godhead. It is equally clear that this intimacy involved becoming "one flesh" (2:24). God made men and women to bond in a one-flesh, husband-wife relationship.[141] Such one-flesh bonding involves physical, emotional, and spiritual intimacy. Eve's first role was as Adam's intimate companion. Her responsibility was to dispel his aloneness.

Eve was Adam's complement.

The second word in Genesis 2:18 which requires some in-depth analysis is the word *helper*. What does it mean that the woman would be the man's helper? Does it mean she was to be a co-laborer with him in the garden harvesting the fruit? Again, we must look to the language of the Old Testament to unlock the meaning of this word. The noun, *helper*, in Hebrew means, "a succor, one who provides assistance."[142] Eve was to be Adam's helper, providing him with assistance. Not just any helper, Eve was to be Adam's "suitable" helper. A suitable helper is, one who is "corresponding to, conspicuous, in front of."[143] When used as an adverb, this word means "opposite."[144] Eve was Adam's complement, his conspicuous opposite. Her second responsibility was to provide Adam with assistance as his equal and conspicuous complement. She was not merely a "fellow fruit picker" with Adam. Together they were royalty, commissioned by God to rule the earth (Gen. 1:26–27).

The first two roles of an authentic woman are to be an intimate

---

141   It is clear from the Genesis 2 account of the creation of Eve that Adam took Eve as his wife. The Hebrew word used in 2:24, 25 is אִשָּׁה ['ishah] "wife (woman belonging to a man)", Brown, Driver, & Briggs, p. 61.

142   עֵזֶר [ēzer] Brown, Driver, & Briggs, p. 740, 741.

143   נֶגֶד [neged] Ibid., p. 617.

144   מִנֶּגֶד [mineged] Ibid., p. 617.

companion and a conspicuous complement to a man. As much as men and women today often function independently of one another in every area, the original design for men and women was for them to form a complementary partnership to rule the earth.

Eve was the mother of all living.

Even prior to the fall of Adam and Eve into sin, God always intended Eve to bear children (cf. Gen. 1:28). The fall brought intensified pain in childbirth (Gen. 3:16). Adam named the woman, Eve, meaning "mother of all living," because she would be the mother of his children (Gen. 3:20). The third role of an authentic woman is to be a mother and bear children for her husband. Genesis 4:1 records the first incidence of sexual relations between a man and woman. The context God established for sexual relations is a committed monogamous, heterosexual marriage. Marriage has always been God's context for reproducing the human race and raising children.

Eve came under Adam's rule.

Not coincidentally, the fall brought with it a change in Adam and Eve's relationship to one another. Eve is told that part of the curse upon her was that she would come under the "rule" of her husband (Gen. 3:16). *Rule* in the Hebrew means, "to reign, have dominion over another."[145] Because of sin and depravity it is clear that distortion of the roles has emerged. The relationship has changed forever. Now Adam would rule Eve by power, coercion, or authority.[146] Submission to the headship of men is the final responsibility of women. Loving headship is God's gracious provision for women in a fallen world. Submission is a wife's righteous response to her

---

[145] מָשַׁל [*mashal*] Ibid., p. 605.
[146] Wayne Grudem, *Evangelical Feminism & Biblical Truth: An Analysis of More than 100 Disputed Questions.* Sisters, OR: Multnomah Publishers, 2004), p. 40.

husband's leadership. Such submission will involve yielding to him as her provider, protector, sanctifier, sacrificer, lover, and leader. The authentic woman will treat her husband with respect (Eph. 5:33). The tempter would push women to the extremes of either usurping the authority of men and functioning as head over them or becoming passive and docile depriving men of the benefit of their wisdom.

True Beauty

God has made women attractive to men. Men desire women and vice versa. Men are visually stimulated and the very sight of women stimulates men. All of that is good and designed by God. He designed men and women to be attracted to one another. Such attraction insures the carrying out of the command to "be fruitful and multiply, and fill the earth" (Gen. 1:28 NASV). God, Himself, is beautiful, says Psalm 27:4, and we are made in His image, beautiful.

Outer Beauty

However, the Bible makes it clear that outer beauty is fleeting and is not to be the basis for how a pure woman relates to a man. He may be initially attracted by the external but an honorable man will stay because of her inner beauty. Beauty fades with time. It is like a flower that withers under the scorching sun (James 1:10–11).

Beauty can be misused for sinful purposes. Ezekiel 16 details that kind of misuse of beauty. Through Ezekiel, the Lord pronounces a scathing rebuke of Jerusalem. He details how He rescued her as an infant and nurtured her from her youth to adulthood. He entered into the covenant of marriage with her and gave her fine clothes to wear, luscious food to eat, and adorned her with fine jewelry. Because she was so beautiful, the Lord made her famous among the nations. But she became corrupted by her beauty and arrogant in her pride. She became a spiritual prostitute with nations. She lusted after their false gods committing abominable rites. Beauty was a snare to Jerusalem. She was beautiful on the outside but ugly on the inside. The same can be true for any woman.

Inner Beauty

God desires more than outer beauty in a woman. He wants her to be beautiful on the inside. What does inner beauty look like? 1 Peter 3:1–6 gives us the best description in the Bible of internal beauty. Peter writes to describe how submissive wives win disobedient husbands. The answer is that they win them through their inner beauty.

She possesses the beauty of true submission.

From 1 Peter 3:1, wives are to be submissive to their husbands (cf. Eph. 5:22–24, Col. 3:18). True submission is submission from the heart, not simply external compliance. False submission is characterized by outer compliance but inner defiance. It is marked by ungodly attitudes of pride and rebellion.

True submission, however, is a beautiful thing. The heart of the woman who possesses it hopes in God, not simply her husband (3:5). The heart of the submissive wife does not fear the outcome of her husband's decisions for she trusts God exclusively (3:6). True submission becomes visible when her husband sees her pure and reverent behavior (cf. Eph. 5:33).[147] True submission of the heart is seen in a "gentle and quiet spirit" (1

---

[147] The phrase in 1 Peter 3:2 is, ἐν φόβῳ ἁγνὴν ἀναστροφὴν ὑμῶν [*en phobō hagnēn avastrophēn humōn*] lit. "in fear pure behavior of you". The disobedient husband observes the reverent, pure behavior of his wife and is drawn to her God. In fact, she witnesses to him by her life not with her lips (1 Pet. 3:1).

Pet. 3:4) that is peacefully trusting God.

She displays the beauty of modesty.

Peter describes the true adornment of a pure woman. He says true adornment is not the outer attire of the body. Women of the world focus their efforts on the external—their hairstyle and color, gold jewelry, and the latest styles of clothing (1 Pet. 3:3). Peter says that is all changing and perishable. It quickly fades away with each new fashion trend. True adornment clothes the inner woman, making her beautiful. Inner beauty is imperishable (1 Pet. 3:4). For the pure woman, her outer attire reflects her inner beauty. Her character, not her body, is her focus. She is a modest woman on the inside and outside. She is a gentle, quiet, submissive, God-fearing woman who respects and honors her husband. Her attire reflects who she is. She is modest in her dress and is not swayed by the changing winds of the culture.

Younger Christian women need to be taught modesty by modest older women—hopefully including their mothers. Titus 2:5 exhorts older women to teach younger women to be pure. This includes purity of dress as well as purity of speech, behavior, and attitude. The attire of the pure woman does not cause men to stumble in their walk with God. Her appearance is not a stumbling block to the gospel; rather she is a stepping stone, helping others find Christ.

How Satan Attacks Purity in Women

Satan attacked Eve. He deceived her (2 Cor. 11:3). He tempted her to doubt God's word and to question God's love. In doing so, he led her into sin and painful consequences. Satan uses that same pattern of deception on women.

He Attacks Their Identity

Many women question what God says of their true identity. They don't know or can't accept that they are a child of God and a daughter of the

"Virginity is not an outdated, outmoded, relic from the Victorian era."

King. They buy Satan's lie that their identity is wrapped up in their appearance. Further, they buy the lie that they need a man to be complete instead of understanding that they are complete in Christ (1 Cor. 1:30, 1 John 2:5). Women often believe the lie that to get and keep a man they need to be sexual with him. They seek to attract attention to their physical bodies in extreme and destructive ways.

God says that sex is to be reserved for marriage (Heb. 13:4). Virginity is highly esteemed by God and should be by those who love Him. God's priests in the Old Testament were forbidden to marry any woman who was not a virgin (Lev. 21:13–14). For a woman entering into marriage not to be a virgin was grounds for divorce (Matt. 1:19).

God's Plan for Singles

Virginity Until Marriage

Virginity is not an outdated, outmoded, relic from the Victorian era. It is God's gracious plan of protection for singles. Virginity is for both single men and single women. I write about this topic here because this chapter deals with the purity of the woman, the bride. The majority of the times the Bible uses the term virgin, it is in the context of the Virgin Daughter of Zion or Virgin Israel. Israel was seen as the virgin bride of God. The church, as the bride of Christ, is composed of men and women.

Virginity as a way of life.

Rosenau and Wilson describe true virginity as more than simply not having sexual union with another. They write:

> We fear for singles who hold physical virginity as "the ultimate goal." How unproductive and hurtful this can be. Instead, the goal should be to build a Christlike character that seeks sexual wholeness and celebrates deep fulfilling intimacy appropriate to each type of relationship. Virginity is the overall lifestyle attitude that guides and protects you along your journey. Physical virginity is a means to the end goal (soul virginity) but is *not* the end itself. It should never be seen as some magical formula for ensuring sexual purity.[148]

True virginity is a way of life that prizes a relationship with God above all else. True virgins are physical, emotional, and spiritual virgins who delight in purity because they treasure Christ above all and focus their lives on Him. They have drawn clear sexual boundaries and make them known during courtship. They practice sexual self-control and rely upon the Holy Spirit to strengthen them during times of temptation. They refuse to masturbate or rationalize masturbation as the "single's version of sex."

Virginity before marriage and faithfulness after marriage is God's plan for human sexuality. It eliminates all worries about contracted sexually-transmitted diseases (STDs), unwanted pregnancies, emotional baggage of guilt, shame, and anger, and separation from God's fellowship and joy.

---

[148] Doug Rosenau & Michael Todd Wilson, *Soul Virgins: Redefining Single Sexuality* (Grand Rapids, MI: Baker Book House, 2006), p. 66.

Hope for Non-Virgins

What hope is there for those who have not prized their virginity? Though there is only one first time, there is hope! They can be emotionally and spiritually healed. Sexual sin has separated the non-virgin from God (Isa. 59:2). The path back to emotional healing and sweet fellowship with God is the same for any sinner: repentance, confession, and the cleansing power of the Holy Spirit (see chapter 6, "How Does a Man Become Pure?"). God delights to forgive and restore sinners who truly repent. He will never turn away from the humble heart who seeks Him (Jer. 32: 40; 1 Pet. 5:5–6).

The Cost to Become a Pure Woman

God's desire for His children is that they be holy as He is holy (Lev. 11:44). He calls us to present our bodies as "a living and holy sacrifice" (Rom. 12:1) and to love Him above all else (Mark 12:30). Pure love of God means obeying Him and walking in purity. Obedience requires submission of our will and this is the cost of becoming a pure woman. It is often hard to submit our will to another, but submitting to Someone who is completely good and loving and who knows us and what is best for us better than we know ourselves, becomes easier and more attractive with practice. The cost of becoming a pure woman is unconditional surrender to the Holy God of the universe.

The cost of becoming a pure woman requires surrender of our perceived right to rule ourselves. It requires death to self and our own agenda. It requires us to value our relationship with Christ above any other relationship in life. In our self-elevating culture, it calls us to be sanctified, set apart, different, humble, and counter cultural. The cost of being pure requires women to essentially be the exact opposite of what popular culture says a woman should be. Pure women do not use their external beauty and/or sex appeal to attract attention to themselves. Pure women are modest so their inner beauty can glorify God.

Obstacles to a Woman's Purity

Purity is dependent upon learning to love, trust, and respect God unconditionally. If a woman does not have a personal, intimate relationship with God through Jesus Christ, purity will be compromised. Obstacles to her purity can come from her lack of knowledge and understanding of who God is and/or her own choice to not submit herself to His authority. Inability to submit may be a result of abuses of authority she experienced as a child and/or a reflection of our culturally rebellious times. Culture lures us away from God and His holy standard. Emotional voids from childhood make a woman especially vulnerable to those who would exploit her sexually. The desire to fill emotionally empty places with God-substitutes, as well as the desire to please people more than God, are tragic obstacles to purity.

Why a Woman Should Become Pure

The most important reason a woman should become pure is identical to the reason a man should become pure—to glorify God. God calls us to be holy as he is holy. Purity characterizes followers of Christ who are spiritually mature. Knowing, understanding, and living in obedience to God and His Word, the woman who walks in purity is first and foremost pleasing to God. Further, a morally pure woman portrays love and respect for herself and others. Understanding her own self-worth as being precious to God and created in His image, she evidences self-respect through being pure. She is a model of purity for the sake of her husband, her children, and others. Through her purity, she honors the Lord, herself, and all women. Her godly example may lead someone to Christ. A woman who walks in purity also walks in freedom and experiences the peaceful fruit of righteousness (Heb. 12:11).

Benefits of Living as a Pure Woman

The woman who walks in purity enjoys the blessings of God and the respect of self and others. She enjoys freedom from guilt, shame, and sexual bondage. She is free to love and serve God and people. She is free to be a blessing to her husband, her children, fellow believers, and unbelievers. She is empowered by the Holy Spirit to nurture without resentment those under her care and she is free to be in biblical harmony with her husband. She is able to be an encouragement to fellow believers and a witness for Christ to unbelievers. She brings joy to the heart of God (3 John v 4).

The Power to Submit with Respect to Her Husband

A woman's ability to submit to her husband flows out of her ability to submit to God. In order for her to be able to biblically submit to her husband, she must first know and understand who God is and allow Him to be in authority over her. Her husband can make this either harder or easier for her. If he does not love her as Christ loved the church, she will be inclined to reject his authority, particularly if she has been hurt by previous authority abuse. If he loves her sacrificially as Christ loved the church, he can make submission attractive. Either way, the power to submit to her husband comes from God. He will bless the woman who submits first to God and then to her husband. As she releases her husband to God's control and chooses to honor and respect him, she will be free of both the need to control him and the desire to resist his authority.

How to Become a Pure Woman

A woman is on her way to becoming pure when her heart's desire is to glorify God. Becoming pure involves deliberate choices that reflect an obedient heart that understands the holiness of God and desires to please Him above all else. She must be pure in her thoughts, words, and deeds. She must be careful to protect her mind from impure input from all outside sources. (No romance novels for her!) Paul instructs believers in this regard, "Whatever is true, whatever is honorable, whatever is right, whatever is pure … let your mind dwell on these things" (Phil. 4:8 NASV). To become pure, a woman must dress modestly and not be a stumbling block to men because of what she is wearing. Her dress should communicate that she is a child of God. Discernment, not fashion alone, will determine her clothing choices.

Purity requires personal salvation and an intimate relationship with the Lord Jesus Christ. It requires daily investment of time in God's Word and in prayer. It requires daily walking with Jesus in obedience to His Word so that time spent with Him is translated into a life of obedience that glorifies Him. To become a pure woman means to fall in love with Jesus and love learning more and more about His heart and character. To become a pure woman means to grow closer and closer to Him each day so there is no room for anything to come between her and her best friend, Jesus.

CHAPTER EIGHT
THE POWER OF A PURE MARRIAGE

Marriage should be honored by all, and the marriage bed kept pure, for God will judge the adulterer and all the sexually immoral.

Hebrews 13:4

God's Purpose and Design for Marriage

Marriage is God's idea. He created Adam and Eve and brought them together. Reflecting on this new relationship, the biblical record sums up marriage by stating, "For this reason a man will leave his father and mother and be united to his wife, and they will become one flesh" (Gen. 2:24). Anthony Hoekema observes that the idea of marriage precedes even Genesis 2:24. He explains, "The injunction to be fruitful and multiply [in Genesis 1:28] implies the institution of marriage, the establishment of which is narrated in the second chapter of Genesis (vv. 18–24)."[149]

The Purpose of Marriage

There are many reasons why couples marry:

(a) love

---

[149]   Hoekema, *Created in God's Image*, p. 14.

(b) escape from parents

(c) pressure from peers, relatives, or others

(d) desire for children

(e) money

(f) lack of sexual self-control

The biblical reason for marriage, however, is to glorify the Lord. Marriages are to reflect the glory of God to a dark world. Because both men and women bear the image of God, both reflect the glory of God. The psalmist declares:

> When I consider your heavens, the work of your fingers,
>
> the moon and the stars, which you have set in place, what
>
> is man that you are mindful of him, the son of man that you
>
> care for him? You made him a little lower than the heavenly
>
> beings and crowned him with glory and honor. You made
>
> him ruler over the works of your hands; you put everything
>
> under his feet. (Ps. 8:3–6)

What is true of husband and wife individually is multiplied when combined. Marriage is the union of two image-bearers that intensifies the brilliance of God's glory within them. Allender and Longman help us understand this concept when they write:

> What does this say about the nature and purpose of
>
> marriage? Simply, the goal of marriage is twofold: to reveal
>
> the glory of God and to enhance the glory of one's spouse.
>
> If I am to love my spouse as God intended, I will recognize
>
> her as an image-bearer of God and will live to enhance
>
> her beauty, her glory, in order to live out the glory of God

... Our spouses are representatives of God. We are called

to delight in and to enhance one another's already present

glory to the glory of God. Our only option in responding to

our spouses is either to glorify or to degrade them.[150]

Man and Woman Created to Be Co-regents of Earth

The original intent of God was for Adam and Eve to be co-regents ruling over the earth and all the creatures on it (Gen. 1:28). This is called the cultural mandate: the command to rule the earth for God. Exercising dominion over all the earth is a confirmation of the fact that people are made in the image of God.[151] Humans are granted dominion as an outcome of being made in the likeness of God (Gen. 1:26). God rules all creation and has given the capacity to rule to his image-bearers. As co-regents prior to the fall, Adam and Eve were king and queen ruling over God's planet (Gen. 1:26, 28; Ps. 8:6–8; Heb. 2:6–8).

God's Design For Marriage

God's original blueprint for marriage in Genesis also provided the standards and parameters for marriage for all time. Though humanity may deviate from God's original design, that does not invalidate the standard. Mankind's deviation from God's standards invites both natural and divine consequences. God's original design for marriage, as described in Genesis 2:24, was for a man to leave father and mother and unite with a woman in

---

[150] Dan Allender & Tremper Longman, *Intimate Allies* (Wheaton, IL: Tyndale House, 1995), p. 22.
[151] Hoekema, p. 78.

a permanent, committed, "one flesh" relationship. God's design is clearly for marriage to be heterosexual in structure. The heterosexual structure of marriage is confirmed in the New Testament: "But since there is so much immorality, each man should have his own wife, and each woman her own husband" (1 Cor. 7:2).

Marriage is a Covenant Relationship

Marriage was designed by God to be a covenant relationship. A marriage covenant is a binding agreement between two people in the presence of God in which conditions are specified and promises are made. To appreciate the biblical view of marriage as a sacred covenant, it is helpful to distinguish between a covenant and a contract. Paul Palmer offers a helpful clarification of the difference between the two:

> Contracts engage the services of people; covenants engage persons. Contracts are made for a stipulated period of time; covenants are forever. Contracts can be broken, with material loss to the contracting parties; covenants cannot be broken, but if violated, they result in personal loss and broken hearts. Contracts are witnessed by people with the state as guarantor; covenants are witnessed by God with God as guarantor.[152]

In the wedding vows they exchange, couples agree to remain faithful to one another through all the circumstances of life when they answer the question, "Wilt thou love him/her, comfort him/her, honor, and keep him/her, in sickness and in health; and, forsaking all others, keep thee only unto him/her so long as ye both shall live?" with "I will." The covenant they enter into

---

[152] Paul E. Palmer, "Christian Marriage: Contract or Covenant?" (*Theological Studies, 33* (4), 1972), p. 639.

binds them in a union of exclusivity and fidelity for the duration of their lives on earth. Concerning the marriage covenant, Macrae writes:

> When a covenant was made in the Old Testament the two parties involved in the agreement would take a living animal and cut it in half from top to bottom. As the animal's blood was shed it symbolized the death of the individual rights of the covenant-makers. The covenant-makers would then walk between two rows of the slain animals body parts symbolizing their union. In a sense the covenant-makers were making a statement that if they broke the conditions of the covenant what happened to these animals would be the fate of the covenant breaker. When God and Abraham made their covenant [Genesis 15:8–21] it was only God who passed between the animals. This was because the two parties were not equal partners in their covenantal relationship.[153]

Leaving and Cleaving

At the heart of the marriage covenant is a commitment between a man and a woman. That commitment is expressed in the form of a covenant between themselves and God and applied by leaving parents and cleaving to one another.[154] In marriage, a husband and wife bond together to form a new social unit, a family. Children don't make a family; they simply expand what already exists. Leaving and cleaving is not merely physical. Leaving involves

---

[153]   Robert A. Macrae, *The Effects of Premarital Heterosexual Behaviors on an Individual's Perspective of the Sexual Relationship in a Christian Marriage* (St. Paul, MN: Bethel Theological Seminary, 2000), p. 29.

[154]   In Gen. 2:24, "cleave", דָּבַק, literally means "to cling, cleave, keep close" together. Brown, Driver, & Briggs, p. 179.

a husband and wife disengaging themselves from their parents physically, emotionally, and spiritually and bonding together physically, emotionally, and spiritually.

Marital Satisfaction in Marriage

Is marriage for our happiness or our holiness? Does God intend marriage to be satisfying or is marriage God's vehicle to cause us to become holy? God delights in marital satisfaction *and* in marital holiness. Yes, God intended marriage to be the vehicle for populating the earth and nurturing children, but He also intended it to be a source of great delight and satisfaction. Marital holiness leads to marital happiness.

Human Marriage Is Modeled After Christ's Relationship to His Church

God intended marriage between a husband and wife to be a reflection of Christ's relationship to the church. In chapter six, the six responsibilities of a pure man were described based upon the six responsibilities Christ has toward His Church. Christ leads (Eph. 5:23), loves (Eph. 5:25), sacrifices (Eph. 5:25), sanctifies (Eph. 5:26–27; John 17:17), provides (John 17:14, 22, 26; Eph. 5:29), and protects (John 17:11–12, 15) His Church. Husbands must love their wives in the same six ways.

Holiness Is Central to Marriage

Holiness is central to Christ's love for His bride. Christ died to make His church holy (Eph. 5:25–26). Only through His blood can she be washed clean from her sins. Hebrews 9:14 says, "How much more, then, will the blood of Christ, who through the eternal Spirit offered himself unblemished to God, cleanse our consciences from acts that lead to death, so that we may serve the living God!" Further in Hebrews, the writer declares, "In fact, the law requires that nearly everything be cleansed with blood, and without the shedding of blood there is no forgiveness" (Heb. 9:22). Now we are exhorted to "draw near to God with a sincere heart in full assurance of faith, having our hearts sprinkled to cleanse us from a guilty conscience and having our bodies washed with pure water" (Heb. 10:22). In our position in Christ, we stand purified and holy before God. The apostle John writes, "But if we walk in the light, as he is in the light, we have fellowship with one another, and the blood of Jesus, his Son, purifies us from all sin" (1 John 1:7). Without holiness, no one will see God (Heb. 12:14).

God uses marriage to make partners holy. The apostle Paul says that marriage is to be a source of sanctification for partners (Eph. 5:27, 1 Thess. 4:3). Marriage is the most intimate of all human relationships. Because of its intimacy, marriage allows partners to see each other under the microscope. God uses this intimacy to shape and mold partners into the image of his Son, Jesus Christ. Allender and Longman comment on this idea, "God's intention for marriage is to grow or subdue each partner in relation to the other in order to draw each—and eventually the marriage itself—to reflect the character of his Son."[155] Further they write that marriage, "… is the relationship where depravity is best exposed and where our dignity is best lived out."[156] In describing holiness in his own marriage, Thomas explains:

> What marriage has done for me is hold up a mirror to my
> sin. It forces me to face myself honestly and consider my
> character flaws, selfishness, and anti-Christian attitudes,
> encouraging me to be sanctified and cleansed and
> to grow in godliness.[157]

---

[155]   Allender and Longman, p. 84.

[156]   Ibid., p. 288.

[157]   Gary Thomas, *Sacred Marriage: What if God Designed Marriage to Make us Holy More than to Make us Happy* (Grand Rapids, MI: Zondervan Publish-

Holiness is central in Christ's marriage to the church and must be central in human marriage.

Marriage Is to Be a Source of Satisfaction

God delights in satisfying his people. In fact, God delights to satisfy every living thing (Ps. 145:16). He satisfies our physical, emotional, and spiritual needs (see Ps. 81:16, 90:14, 91:16, 132:15; Isa. 55:2, 58:11; Jer. 31:14, 25). Is it any wonder that God delights in making marriage a source of satisfaction to His people?

King Solomon understood that marriage was to be satisfying. In Proverbs 5:18–19 he exhorts his readers to be faithful to one's wife. He uses several metaphors to describe the delights of marriage as he writes, "May your fountain be blessed, and may you rejoice in the wife of your youth. A loving doe, a graceful deer—may her breasts satisfy you always, may you ever be captivated by her love." Solomon calls his readers to sexual exclusivity. He calls the sexual relationship of a married couple a "fountain" (in 5:15 he called it a "cistern" and "well," in 5:16, "springs" and "streams") because it refreshes their souls. This is a good reason to "rejoice in the wife of your youth." She is to be the exclusive focus of your sexual energy, not "strangers" (5:17). Solomon is using the metaphors cistern, well, springs, streams, and fountain—all water-carrying, life-giving vessels—to refer to one's wife. Water is symbolic of fertility and life-giving.[158] As one who could bear children, wives are life-giving.

Solomon calls the breasts of one's wife a "loving doe, a graceful deer." In what way are breasts like deer? The same question was asked by Longman as he pondered Song of Songs 4:5. In describing this similar

---

ing House, 2000), p. 93.

[158] Brown, et al., p. 565.

passage, written by the same author (Solomon), using similar language, Longman writes, "The *fawn/gazelle* was known for a variety of qualities including speed, sleekness, and sensuality. Speed hardly seems a fitting comparison with a woman's breasts, but certainly an attractiveness of form is ... Are we to picture them from the rear then? That is, as they stick their heads into the sweet smell of the flowers, their rounded rumps with their small tails may remind the poet of breasts with their protruding nipples."[159] Her breasts, then, are extolled as a source of sensuality (an erogenous zone) and sleek and graceful of form. A wife's breasts are to satisfy her husband all his days so much so that he is never drawn to another. Solomon exhorts his readers to marital exclusivity when he declares, "May you ever be captivated by her love" (Prov. 5:19). Kidner says of the word *captivated* that "as it can also describe the effects of strong drink (Prov. 20:1; Is. 28:7) it might be rendered in verses 19 and 20 'be intoxicated.' "[160] Within marriage, the sexual relationship is to be so satisfying and bonding, the love so intoxicating that infidelity is unthinkable.

Sexuality and the Single Christian

What about singles? If marriage is God's gift to mankind, what provision is there for those who do not marry? The Bible speaks to the needs of singles. The single state is commended as preferable to marriage because of the ability of singles to live a less-troubled, less-concerned-about-the-world life and give undistracted devotion to God (cf. 1 Cor. 7:28–35). Nevertheless, the apostle Paul tells the unmarried Corinthians:

Now to the unmarried and the widows I say: It is good for

---

[159] Tremper I. Longman, *Song of Songs* (Grand Rapids, MI: William B. Eerdmans Publishing Company, 2001), p. 147.
[160] Kidner, p. 71.

them to stay unmarried, as I am. But if they cannot control themselves, they should marry, for it is better to marry than to burn with passion. (1 Cor. 7:8–9)

What does Paul mean by the phrase "better to marry than to burn with passion"?[161] Most commentaries agree with the NIV's addition of "with passion" to the phrase under consideration. Ryrie and Morris note that "to burn" means to be aflame "with passion" or "sexual desire."[162] Singles burning with sexual passion clearly do not have the gift of celibacy (cf. 1 Cor. 7:7). Better for them to marry than become sexually immoral. So marriage is God's preventative strategy against sexual immorality for singles.

The Bible exhorts all Christians, whether single or married, to practice sexual self-control (1 Cor. 7:6, 9). Self-control, not masturbation or fornication, is God's provision for singles. Self-control, not masturbation of adultery, is God's provision for those who marry. Self-control and regular sexual intercourse protect a marriage against Satan's temptations to be sexually unfaithful (1 Cor. 7:5).

Keeping the Marriage Bed Pure

What does the writer of Hebrews 13:4 mean when he tells us that "marriage should be honored by all, and the marriage bed kept pure, for God will judge the adulterer and all the sexually immoral"? What is the "marriage bed" and what does it mean to keep the marriage bed "pure"? The Greek does not include the word *marriage* but simply says "the bed."[163] The writer of Hebrews is using the word *bed* metaphorically. He is not describing the

---

[161] The NIV has added the words "with passion." The original Greek is simply κρεῖττον γάρ ἐστιν γαμῆσαι ἢ πυροῦσθαι [*kreitton gar estin gamēsai ē purousthai*], "for it is better to marry than to burn."

[162] Ryrie, p. 1735; Morris, p. 108.

[163] ἡ κοίτη [*hē koitē*] "the bed," Engl. "coitus"

literal bed on which a couple sleeps. Rather, he is using the metaphor of a bed to represent the sexual relationship within marriage. Bed is a most fitting metaphor, for it is the typical location of sexual union within marriage. The writer is saying that the sexual relationship within marriage must be guarded from anything that would defile it.

From the context of the verse, it is clear that adultery and sexual immorality render the marriage bed impure. God will judge those who practice such sexual impurity. Keeping a pure marriage bed focuses on the sexual side of marriage. Only sexual exclusivity and fidelity can keep the marriage bed pure.

The Greek word *amiantos* translated in the NIV as "pure" is used four times in the New Testament. Arndt and Gingrich say it means, "undefiled or pure in a religious and moral sense."[164] *Amiantos* is not the most commonly used word for pure in the New Testament. Typically, the New Testament writers use *hagnos* (eight times) or *katharos* (25 times) to express the idea of purity, cleanness, or sacredness.[165] Why did God move the writer of Hebrews to choose *amiantos*? If God had meant pure in Hebrews 13:4 to be understood as freedom from physical or moral pollution, he would probably have chosen *katharos*. If God had meant pure to be understood as religious sacredness, sanctification or holiness, he would probably have chosen *hagnos*. God chose *amiantos* to convey the idea that the sexual relationship within marriage must be kept unspoiled, unpolluted. The NIV elsewhere translates *amiantos* as "keep from being *polluted* [italics added] by the world" (James 1:27) and "an inheritance that can never perish, *spoil* [italics added] or fade" (1 Pet. 1:4).

---

[164] ἀμίαντος Arndt and Gingrich, p. 45.
[165] ἁγνός, καθαρός W. F. Moulton, & A. S. Geden, (Eds.). *A Concordance to the Greek Testament* (Edinburgh, Scotland: T & T Clark, 1963).

Hauck states that *amiantos* was used by Plutarch to describe "the virginal purity of the Vestals." He goes on to say that in the Septuagint, it occurs five times where it is translated "a few times for sexual purity."[166]

The marriage bed (the sexual relationship) is not necessarily pure in and of itself. It is only pure when a pure (sexually faithful, married) couple occupies it. For such couples, sexual union within marriage is blessed by God and declared pure.

The Attack on Marriage

Satan hates marriage. It stands to reason that if Satan hates God and anything that is God's will, Satan hates marriage because God designed it. Marriage is a picture of Christ and the church and is God's will for mankind. Accordingly, Satan attacks marriage in a number of ways:

(a) by undermining it through cohabitation

(b) by deconstructing it through same-sex marriage

(c) by devaluing it through "open" or "starter" marriages

(d) by defiling it through infidelity

P.O.S.S.L.Q. or Cohabitation

The United States Census Bureau calls them "POSSLQs," that is, "persons of opposite sex sharing living quarters." Most call it cohabitation. This may be between people of the same sex in a platonic or a homosexual relationship, but most often it is two heterosexuals living together. Research indicates that in the USA, 8.1 percent of coupled households are made up of unmarried, heterosexual partners. Why are couples living together without marrying? Many have seen their parents divorce and are afraid to marry. Some

---

[166] Friedrich Hauck, ἀμίαντος, In G. Kittel, & G. Friedrich (Eds.), *Theological Dictionary of the New Testament* (G. W. Bromiley, Trans., Vol. 4) (Grand Rapids, MI: William B. Eerdmans Publishing Company, 1983), p. 647.

are "commitment phobic" and are afraid of the long-term implications of marriage. Others enjoy the "no strings attached" sexual relationship.

Is cohabitation a good or bad thing for society? What is God's view of it? "Cohabitation is here to stay," says David Popenoe, a Rutgers sociology professor and co-author of *The State of our Unions 2005,* a report analyzing the census findings. "I don't think it's good news, especially for children," he says. "As society shifts from marriage to cohabitation—which is what's happening—you have an increase in family instability." Cohabiting couples have twice the breakup rate of married couples, the report's authors say. And in the USA, 40 percent bring kids into these often-shaky live-in relationships. The USA has the lowest percentage among Western nations of children who grow up with both biological parents, 63 percent, the report says.

"The United States has the weakest families in the Western world because we have the highest divorce rate and the highest rate of solo parenting," Popenoe says.[167] Cohabitation undermines marriage.

What does the Bible say about cohabitation? The term the Bible uses for non-celibate cohabitation is fornication. Fornication is the same word as sexual immorality, *porneia.* Fornication is engaging in sexual intercourse outside of the marriage covenant. It is uniformly condemned in the Bible as a sin. For example, 1 Corinthians 6:9–10 declares, "Do you not know that the wicked will not inherit the kingdom of God? Do not be deceived: Neither the sexually immoral [fornicators] nor idolaters nor adulterers nor male prostitutes nor homosexual offenders ... will inherit the kingdom of God." Why does God condemn fornication? Because He loves us so much that He wants to

---

[167] Sharon Jayson, *Divorce Declining, but So is Marriage* (Retrieved July 23, 2008, http://www.usatoday.com/news/nation/2005-07-18-cohabit-divorce_x.htm, 2005).

protect us from the physical, emotional, and spiritual harm of premarital sex.

Cohabitation is an especially "bad deal" for women. In the Bible, women who cohabited with a man were called concubines.[168] Concubines were considered secondary or inferior wives. They lived with men, even calling them husbands. They had all the responsibilities of wives including bearing them children, but had none of the legal rights of wives. A writ of divorcement detailing the offenses of a wife was required of a husband divorcing his wife. Not so for a concubine. She could be put out without any written grounds. Her children had no inheritance rights or legal standing in the courts. "Christianity restores the sacred institution of marriage to its original character, and concubinage is ranked with fornication and adultery (Matt. 19:5; 1 Cor. 7:2).[169] Even so, today's cohabitation is producing a whole new generation of concubines.

Same Sex Marriage

Homosexual behavior is uniformly condemned throughout the pages of Scripture. Leviticus 18:22 calls it an "abomination," and Leviticus 20:13 says that homosexual behavior under Old Testament law is punishable by death. In the New Testament it is called unrighteous (1 Cor. 6:9), shameful, unnatural, dishonoring, indecent, degrading, and a perversion (Rom. 1:24–27). In the context of Romans 1:18–3:20, Lewis and Demarest comment on the seriousness of this sin: " ... homosexuality is particularly odious, since it

---

[168] פִּלֶגֶשׁ [*pilegesh*] "concubine," Brown, et al., p. 811. It is interesting the close connection in Hebrew between the noun for concubine and the verb for "split, divide," פָּלַג. Could it be that concubines were often sources of division and splits within families? The Biblical conflict of Sarah and Hagar, the concubine, is one such example.

[169] Merrill F. Unger, *Unger's Bible Dictionary*, (Chicago, IL: Moody Press, 1977), p. 217.

represents a perversion of his purpose for the race as male and female."[170] Can homosexuals be forgiven and washed clean of their sins? Yes! The Corinthian Church included former homosexuals who were washed, sanctified, and justified by the Lord Jesus Christ (1 Cor. 6:9–11). God loves homosexuals but hates their sin. God's love, however, is not what many homosexuals are after. They want equality in every way with heterosexuals. Gene Veith explains this:

> It is not enough for many homosexuals to hear that
> they can find forgiveness for their sin in the grace
> of God through Jesus Christ. Rather, homosexuals
> want to hear that they are not sinners, that they do
> not need forgiveness for what they do.[171]

What happens then when homosexuals want to marry? What impact does homosexual marriage have on society? As many heterosexuals say, "What difference does it make? Everyone should have the freedom to do whatever he wants. After all, it doesn't affect me!" In an insightful article, Veith writes:

> If Sarasohn [lesbian author he quotes] is right, this means
> that the institution of marriage has become functionally
> and culturally obsolete. People still want to get married.
> But because marriage has no particular purpose, people
> can define and practice their marriages in any way they
> choose.[172]

Homosexual marriage is wrong. It is a sinful, willful, violation of

---

[170] Lewis & Demarest, p. 2:202.
[171] Gene E. Veith, "Sex Appeal: How a Branch of Islam Wants to Convert the West," *World*, July 26/August 2, 2008, *23, 29.*
[172] Gene E. Veith, "Uncommon Bond: Family Collapse Opens a Door for Totalitarianism," *World*, July 12/19, 2008, *23, 29.*

God's design for marriage based upon a sinful sexual practice. Homosexual marriage deconstructs marriage by, in effect, saying, "it doesn't matter who you marry. It is up to the individuals involved to define marriage however they choose. Because we reject God's definition of marriage, marriage has become an empty term, devoid of meaning and purpose." Such thinking will ultimately lead to the demise of marriage as we know it. God's great gift of marriage will have become irrelevant and obsolete. Matthew 24:38 says that people will still marry even until the time of Christ's return, but marriage will have become an empty social institution. It will be a hollow excuse for a party or to receive gifts. It will no longer be a sacred covenant that reflects Christ and His Church.

When that happens, society will have lost something precious, a pearl of great price. The consequences for society include the loss of stability and morality. Children, who look to their parents for an example of manhood and womanhood, will suffer most. The fabric holding society together will have shredded.

Monogamous versus Open Marriage

Gangel states, " ... both male and female were expected to follow God's monogamous pattern. The human race had hardly begun its expansion before we see in Lamech the first distortion of God's monogamous plan (Gen. 4:19)."[173] God's original design was for one man to marry one woman. Polygamy was never his plan for marriage. Neither was the post-sexual revolution version called "open marriage." The American Heritage Dictionary defines "open marriage" as "a marriage in which the partners agree that each is free to engage in extramarital relationships." Open marriage is simply a

---

[173]   Kenneth Gangel, "Toward a Biblical Theology of Marriage and Family" *Journal of Psychology and Theology, 5* (1, 2, 3, & 4), 1977, p. 56.

contemporary term for mutual adultery and adultery is uniformly condemned in the Bible as a sin (Exod. 20:14, Heb. 13:4).

Permanent versus Starter Marriage

God's design for marriage is that husband and wife enter into a permanent, not a temporary, union, even as God is permanently united to his people. Such permanency is seen in Genesis 2:24 in the term *cleave* and in the one-flesh union established. Jesus reinforced the concept of permanence in marriage when he declared in Matthew 19:6, "So they are no longer two, but one. Therefore what God has joined together, let man not separate." God is the only one who can cause the two to become one. Jesus warns against permitting man to untie what God has united.

The contemporary western world is experimenting with variations of the biblical concept of marriage. One of those variations is "starter" marriage in which a couple marries knowing that if it doesn't work out divorce is always an option. Sometimes called "practice" or "rehearsal" marriage, the definition of a starter marriage is, "a first marriage that lasts only a short time and that ends in a clean (i.e., no kids, no property, no acrimony) divorce."[174] In a starter marriage, the couple marries for a short period of time, typically five years or less, remains childless, divorces, and then finds and marries their permanent partners. Proponents of starter marriage claim that it demystifies marriage for young couples, helps them gain an understanding of the rigors of marriage, and prepares them for a lasting, lifelong union in the future. Because divorce has become acceptable to society, marriage is simply viewed as another experience to make one happy. Psychologist Linda Mintle says of

---

[174] Pamela Paul, *The Starter Marriage and the Future of Matrimony* (New York, NY: Random House Trade Paperbacks., 2003), p. 4.

starter marriage, "Marriage is reduced to clothing status—you try it on for a while, if it doesn't fit, discard it and look for a new coat."[175] Starter marriage denigrates the permanence and sacredness God intended marriage to be. It reduces marriage from a binding covenant to a legal contract that can easily be dissolved. Open and starter marriages devalue marriage.

Causes, Consequences, and Cure of Sexual Infidelity

Marriage is designed to be an exclusive relationship between one man and one woman. Sexual infidelity involves betrayal of the marriage at the highest levels. It is a betrayal of one's spouse, a betrayal of oneself and one's own promises, a betrayal of the relationship, and a betrayal of God. The marital vows exchanged at the wedding bound the couple in a covenantal relationship with one another. Understood within that covenant is the vow to sexual exclusivity. Any breach of sexual exclusivity by one spouse or the other is considered betrayal, infidelity, and adultery. Whether the breach of sexual exclusivity takes the form of an offline sexual affair, an online sexual affair (cybersex), employing a prostitute, viewing pornography, or telephone sex, all *feel* the same to the betrayed partner. Though there are differences in the degree of woundedness, all sinful sexual behaviors are viewed as betrayals, violations of wedding vows, and an annihilation of trust. Partners overwhelmingly felt that cyber affairs were as emotionally painful to them as live or offline affairs. Many agree that the dishonesty, secrecy, and deception

---

[175] Linda S. Mintle, *A New Trend: Starter Marriages* (Retrieved June 18, 2005, from http://www.cbn.com/LivingTheLife/Features/DrLindaHelps/StarterMarriages.asp, 2005).

were the most painful parts of the infidelity.[176]

The causes of sexual infidelity.

The causes of sexual infidelity are varied and differ by situation. The most common surface-level causes are:

(a) individualistic vulnerabilities such as boredom in the marriage, need for variety and excitement, thrill-seeking, and reclamation of fading youth

(b) marital problems such as anger at spouse, finding emotional intimacy outside of the primary relationship, falling in love with someone else, diminished frequency of sexual intercourse in the marriage, physical disability or sickness of spouse, and marital dissatisfaction

(c) societal/cultural influences such as the double standard in many Mediterranean cultures and the expectation of infidelity in the entertainment industry[177]

Deeper causes include:

(a) unhealthy family-of-origin dynamics (modeling, abuse, roles, rules)

(b) lack of intimacy (physical, emotional, and spiritual) in the primary relationship

(c) defective character such as pathological lying, and narcissism

(d) sin of turning sex into a spiritual idol and looking to it instead of

---

[176] Jennifer Schneider, "Effects of Cybersex Addiction on the Family: Results of a Survey" (*Journal of Sexual Addiction & Compulsivity, 7*, 2000), pp. 31-58; Jennifer Schneider, Deborah Corley, & Richard Irons, "Surviving Disclosure of Infidelity: Results of an International Survey of 164 Recovering Sex Addicts and Partners" (*Journal of Sexual Addiction & Compulsivity, 5*, 1998), pp. 189-217.

[177] Sharon P. Glass, *Causes of Infidelity* (Retrieved July 21, 2005, from http://www.shirleyglass.com/reflect_infidelity4.htm, 2003).

God to meet needs

 (e) fear of rejection, aging, etc.

 (f) false beliefs (entitlement, double standard, sex and love are separate, independent issues)

 (g) sexual addiction

 (h) lack of monogamous values.

 For sexual infidelity to occur, four conditions must be present—dissatisfaction, fantasy, opportunity, and values. Values are the "trump card," for though a marriage may be dissatisfying, though a spouse may fantasize about what it would be like to be with someone else, and even if the opportunity to do that presented itself, a partner's commitment to monogamy or to not hurting their spouse or to not sinning against God will keep him/her faithful. Biblical values provide moral boundaries for a marriage.[178]

 Marital satisfaction and coital (sexual) satisfaction are the two most likely variables in predicting infidelity. Marital satisfaction seems to be more of a factor for women and coital satisfaction for men. Men tend to compartmentalize and separate sex from love. Thus, a man may contend that he loves his wife and rates his marital satisfaction high, all the while maintaining a long-term sexual affair. Women tend to connect sex with the relationship, such that if the relationship is disconnected the marital satisfaction is low. Men have sexual affairs, women emotional affairs.[179] Infidelity defiles marriage.

---

[178]   Ibid.; Sharon P. Glass, *Shattered Vows: Getting Beyond Betrayal* (Retrieved July 21, 2005, from Smart Marriages: http://www.smartmarriages.com/glass.html, 1998).

[179]   Glass, 1998; Anthony P. Thompson, "Extramarital Sex: A review of the Research Literature" (*The Journal of Sex Research, 19* (1), 1983), pp. 1-22.

The consequences of sexual infidelity.

The primary casualty of sexual unfaithfulness in a marriage is trust. Infidelity, whatever form it takes, is a violation of the marriage covenant. The betrayed spouse is traumatized by the revelation and loses trust in his or her partner. The world they had come to believe was real and safe has been shattered, and the emotional trauma is overwhelming. The discovery of marital infidelity is devastating, because it shatters basic assumptions about the security expected in committed relationships. Marriages operate on a "truth bias," believing that one's partner's word is truth unless there is a history of lying and deception. Rebuilding trust in the marriage is a major component to healing from infidelity.

Other consequences include the emotional impact infidelity has on the wounded partner. Many wounded partners experience damaged self-esteem, hurt, betrayal, abandonment, devastation, loneliness, shame, isolation, humiliation, rage, and jealousy. The sexual relationship of the couple suffers. Wounded spouses tend to lose interest in sex with the betraying partner and report being repulsed by their partner's sexual activities. Many feel unable to compete with computer images. Sometimes wounded partners attempt to increase the sexual activities in an attempt to "win back" the betrayer. This response rarely works. Others issue threats. That also does not work to promote change. Spiritually, the wounded partner either runs to God for help, ıargaining with God, or grows angry with God for allowing this to occur in the marriage.[180]

The loss of trust, the emotional toll, the sexual upheaval may become too much to overcome. The final consequence is that some marriages do not survive infidelity and end in divorce. For others, infidelity, whether online or offline, cyber or real, becomes the catalyst for change.

The cure for infidelity.

What has to happen to overcome infidelity in a marriage? Is there a cure? Infidelity can be healed. First, the betrayer needs to be honest and admit the infidelity without justification. Trust must be rebuilt. To cover up, blame, excuse, deny, rationalize, or lie will only prolong the agony. Second, full disclosure of the story must take place. The wounded spouse needs to determine how much information he or she needs to know at any one time. Typically, disclosure is progressive over a period of time rather than a one-time, overwhelming "information dump." Because of the secrecy and deception surrounding the infidelity, the wounded spouse typically wants to know how, why, where, when, and with whom this happened. The betrayer needs to provide as much information as is being asked.

Third, the betrayer needs to take responsibility for the choices he or she has made, regardless of the problems that pre-existed in the marriage. The

---

[180] Laurie Hall, *An Affair of the Mind: One Woman's Courageous Battle to Salvage her Family from the Devastation of Pornography* (Wheaton, IL: Tyndale House, 1996); Jennifer Schneider, *The New 'Elephant in the Living Room': Effects of Compulsive Cybersex Behaviors on the Spouse,* In Alvin Cooper (Ed.), *Sex and the Internet: A Guide Book for Clinicians* (New York: Brunner-Routledge, 2002), pp. 169-186; Schneider, Corley, & Irons, "Surviving Disclosure of Infidelity: Results of an International Survey of 164 Recovering Sex Addicts and Partners" (*Journal of Sexual Addiction & Compulsivity,* 5, 1998), pp. 189-217.

infidelity cannot be justified. Fourth, the betrayer must humbly repent, confess their sin to God and their spouse and ask for forgiveness. Both partners must be able to grieve over the hurt that has occurred. Fifth, boundaries must be put in place to restore safety to the marriage. Those boundaries will vary depending on the type of sexual infidelity. For skin-to-skin sexual infidelity, contact with the affair partner must be cut off and the affair completely ended. The wounded partner must be part of hearing and seeing the relationship severed. In the case of cyber affairs, the relationship with the affair partner must end and boundaries around the use of the computer put in place. The wounded partner should not become the "sexual police" monitoring the betrayer. The betrayer bears responsibility for confronting and gaining control of his or her behavior.

Sixth, therapy, both individual and conjoint, must be initiated. Therapy for him, if he is the betrayer, should include Every Man's Battle For Purity, the men's purity ministry. Individual therapy for her, if she is the wounded partner, should include helping her look at possible co-dependency or addiction-enabling behaviors. She should also be encouraged to join a Women of Truth group, the purity ministry for wives, for support and healing. A couples group will help them work together on the marriage. Seventh, after sufficient healing has occurred, the couple should be encouraged to renew their wedding vows and form a new covenant. This should be done in the presence of a pastor and can be done as simply or elaborately as desired.[181]

A couple will know they have healed from infidelity when they are able to write their history and include the affair as part of it. They have co-created the story of what they've been through together. Although the

---

[181] Debra Laaser, personal communication, July 11, 2005; Elsie Woolf, personal communication, July 22, 2005.

innocence and naiveté of the old relationship are gone forever, a new, stronger union can be the result.[182]

The Value of Marital Fidelity

Believing that engaging in sexual sin outside of the marriage covenant is infidelity and a breach of the covenant vows, one of the goals of a purity ministry is to restore marital fidelity. Why is marital fidelity important to a marriage?

Marital Fidelity Is Biblical

God is faithful to His people, promising, "Obey me and do everything I command you, and you will be my people, and I will be your God" (Jer. 11:4). One of the underlying principles of God's relationship with His people in both Old and New Testaments is that He is a faithful, promise-keeping God (cf. Josh. 21:45, 23:14; 1 Kings 8:56; Ps. 145:13; 2 Cor. 1:20). He expects no less from His people.

As previously mentioned, Genesis 2:24 establishes God's intention that marriage last for a lifetime. Jesus Christ quotes the same passage in Matthew 19:5–6 and affirms the permanency of marriage. The writer of Hebrews says, "Marriage should be honored by all, and the marriage bed kept pure, for God will judge the adulterer and all the sexually immoral" (Heb. 13:4). The Bible declares that God honors those who are faithful to their marriage vows and partners. Proverbs 5:15, 18 declare, "Drink water from your own cistern, running water from your own well ... May your fountain be blessed, and may you rejoice in the wife of your youth." In fact, Proverbs 5–7 focus on the folly of being seduced by the adulteress. Malachi powerfully states God's position on marital fidelity. In response to Israel's plaintiff cry

---

[182]   Glass, 1998.

that God was no longer paying attention to their prayers or accepting their sacrifices, the Lord declares:

> You ask, "Why?" It is because the LORD is acting as the
> witness between you and the wife of your youth, because
> you have broken faith with her, though she is your partner,
> the wife of your marriage covenant.
> Has not the LORD made them one? In flesh and spirit they
> are his. And why one? Because he was seeking godly
> offspring. So guard yourself in your spirit, and do not break
> faith with the wife of your youth.
> "I hate divorce," says the LORD God of Israel, "and I hate
> a man's covering himself with violence as well as with his
> garment," says the LORD Almighty (Mal. 2:14–16).

The Bible never approves of sexuality outside of marriage. Quite the opposite, it condemns it. Sexuality was designed by God to be exclusively between a husband and wife within the bonds of marriage. Any other sexual relationship by either party, even self sex, is a violation of the one-flesh nature of marriage (Eph. 5:31) and a violation of the marriage vows to be exclusive to one another (1 Cor. 7:2). The apostle Paul describes marital exclusivity this way:

> But since there is so much immorality, each man should
> have his *own* wife, and each woman her *own* husband.
> The husband should fulfill his marital duty to his wife, and
> likewise the wife to her husband. The wife's body does not
> belong to her alone but also to her husband. In the same
> way, the husband's body does not belong to him alone but

also to his wife (1 Cor. 7:2–4, emphasis mine).

Marital Fidelity Provides Security and Safety

Marriage was meant to be a source of security. It is interesting that when Naomi advises Ruth (Ruth 3:1), she speaks of the importance of "finding a home."[183] Keil and Delitzsch say the Hebrew word for home "signifies the condition of a peaceful life, a peaceful and well-secured condition, a secure life under the guardian care of a husband."[184] Of Naomi's implication, Smith explains, "Rest, like the similar word in 1:9, implies the security of marriage."[185] Naomi is urging Ruth to seek Boaz for a husband, for in so doing she will find the security of marriage (see Ruth 3:2–5).

Faithfulness within marriage provides many benefits to both partners. Husbands and wives can defend each other and their children. It ensures that each partner can count on the other to be there in good times and bad. It affords both partners physical and emotional security. It allows them to count on each other. It provides security for the children. Marital fidelity allows the children to find their security in their mother and father.

Marital fidelity also provides safety for both partners and their children. It is nearly impossible for a couple to become infected with a sexually transmitted disease (STD) if both marry as virgins and remain sexually faithful to one another for the life of their marriage. Marital fidelity also ensures that the children will not be exposed to a boy- or girlfriend or stepparent who is a predator.

---

[183]   The Hebrew word מְנוּחָה, translated "home" is often rendered "rest or quiet," Brown, et al. p. 630

[184]   Keil and Delitsch, *Joshua, Judges, Ruth, 1 & 2 Samuel,* p. 483.

[185]   Louise P. Smith, *The Book of Ruth* (Vol. 2) (Nashville, TN: Abingdom-Cokesbury Press, 1953), p. 844.

Marital Vows Are Meant to Be Kept

Marital fidelity is verbalized in the form of marriage vows. God takes vows seriously. In the Old Testament when God's people made a vow they were expected to keep it. To do otherwise was to sin. Deuteronomy 23:21–23 expresses God's expectations:

> If you make a vow to the LORD your God, do not be slow
> to pay it, for the LORD your God will certainly demand it of
> you and you will be guilty of sin. But if you refrain from
> making a vow, you will not be guilty. Whatever your lips
> utter you must be sure to do, because you made your vow
> freely to the LORD your God with your own mouth.

In Numbers 30:2, God says, "When a man makes a vow to the LORD or takes an oath to obligate himself by a pledge, he must not break his word but must do everything he said." Why must he not break his word? Because vows are verbal promises. To break them is to lie, for it is failure to keep one's promise. It is a violation of the ninth commandment by giving a false testimony (cf. Exod. 20:16). Keil and Delitzsch comment that a vow "was a promise made by any one to dedicate and give his own person, or a portion of his property, to the Lord for averting some danger and distress, or for bringing to his possession some desired earthly good."[186]

Jesus emphasized the significance of words when he declared, "But I tell you that men will have to give account on the day of judgment for every careless word they have spoken. For by your words you will be acquitted, and

---

[186] C. F. Keil & Franz Delitzsch, *The Pentateuch* (In C. F. Keil & F. Delitzsch, *Commentary on the Old Testament* (J. Martin, Trans., Vol. 1). Grand Rapids, MI, n.d.), p. 480. The Hebrew noun for vow, נֶדֶר, say Keil and Delitzsch, is a "positive vow, or promise to give or sanctify any part of one's property to the Lord" (p. 223).

by your words you will be condemned" (Matt. 12:36–37). Repeatedly, the New Testament warns against lying and affirms speaking truth (cf. Col. 3:9; Rom. 9:1; 2 Cor. 4:2; 1 Tim. 2:7; 1 John 1:8). Like the Old Testament, the New Testament places a heavy emphasis on truth telling and keeping one's word.

Marriage vows are universal. In every culture and every age, men and women exchange marital vows with one another. Invariably those vows include promises of exclusivity and faithfulness. Whether couples speak words such as, "for better, for worse, for richer for poorer, in sickness and in health, to love and to cherish, until death us do part, according to God's holy ordinance; and thereto I plight thee my troth" or words to that effect, the vows they make are promises to be faithful in all the circumstances of life and to commit themselves exclusively to one another. God expects them to keep their vows.

Why does a purity ministry emphasize keeping marriage vows? Because married men who have been sexually immoral have violated their marriage vows. When they exchanged vows on their wedding day, each partner understood the other to be vowing fidelity and sexual exclusivity. Each expected all sexuality to be exclusively confined to the marriage. Each expected the other to keep their vows. Sexual immorality is the breaking of the marriage vows. It shatters trust in the relationship. Sexual immorality destroys the sexual exclusivity of the marriage, for now one partner has been unfaithful to the other. This is one reason why married men in a purity ministry are urged to renew their marriage vows.

Jesus' Definition of Adultery

Lust Is Adultery of the Heart

Marital vows are broken through adultery. But is adultery only the physical act of sexual intercourse with someone other than one's spouse? Not according to Jesus Christ. He told the multitude in His Sermon on the Mount:

> You have heard that it was said, "Do not commit adultery."
> But I tell you that anyone who looks at a woman lustfully
> has already committed adultery with her in his heart. If your
> right eye causes you to sin, gouge it out and throw it away
> (Matt. 5:27–30).

Jesus taught the multitude that their righteousness must exceed the false standards taught by the Pharisees (Matt. 5:20). As D. M. Lloyd-Jones notes:

> The contrast, therefore, is not between the law given
> through Moses and the teaching of the Lord Jesus Christ; it
> is a contrast, rather, between the false interpretation of the
> law of Moses, and the true presentation of the law given
> by our Lord Himself ... [Regarding Matthew 5:27–30] the
> Pharisees and scribes had reduced the commandment which
> prohibits adultery to the mere physical act of adultery; and
> again they imagined that as long as they were not actually
> guilty of the act itself, the commandment had nothing to
> say to them and they were perfectly innocent as far as it
> was concerned... Once more they had taken the letter of the
> law and reduced it to one particular matter, and thereby had

:d it.[187]

lid not *elevate* the standard of the law. He clarified the true, righteous standards of the law from the false understanding of the law taught by the Pharisees. He called men from mere external obedience to obedience from the heart. Adultery, then, is more than the physical act of sexual unfaithfulness. It is the heart that prompts a lustful look at a woman other than one's wife. It is adultery of the heart and is every bit as damning as physical adultery.

What is lust?

What is lust, and when does looking become lusting? The word for look in Matthew 5:28 means to "look intentionally and continually."[188] As MacArthur notes, "In this usage, the idea is not that of an incidental or involuntary glance but of intentional and repeated gazing."[189] Lust in Matthew 5:28 means "to desire, long for."[190] It is punctiliar or instantaneous in action. Lust is a one-time, lingering, continuous, longing look that flows from an adulterous heart. It is a covetous look, for it desires what does not belong to it. It is an adulterous look for it flows from a heart that is not committed to being a faithful, "one woman" or "one man" heart (cf. 1 Tim. 3:2, 12, 5:9; Titus 1:6). The heart informs the mind how to interpret what the eyes have seen.

An example of this type of adulterous look is described in 2 Samuel 11:2–3. "One evening David got up from his bed and walked around on the

---

[187] D. Martyn Lloyd-Jones, *Studies in the Sermon on the Mount* (Grand Rapids, MI: William B. Eerdmans Publishing Company, 1976), p. 194, 204.

[188] Βλέπων [*blepōn*] in Matt. 5:28 is a present, active participle, which indicates continuous action, i.e. "looking, gazing, ever gawking," Arndt & Gingrich, pp. 142, 143.

[189] John MacArthur, *Matthew 1-7* (Chicago, IL: Moody Press, 1985), p. 302.

[190] ἐπιθυμῆσαι [*epithumēsai*] is an aorist infinitive, Arndt & Gingrich, p. 293.

roof of the palace. From the roof he saw a woman bathing. The woman was very beautiful, and David sent someone to find out about her..." King David did not simply look at Bathsheba; he lusted after her. How do we know it was lust? Because, though married to numerous wives (2 Sam. 5:13), David saw and desired another man's wife with the clear intent of sexual gratification. That is lust. Most people don't act on their lustful looks, but David did. Although he knew that she was the wife of Uriah (2 Sam. 11:3), one of his mighty men, that did not stop David (or Bathsheba) from sexually sinning. David's look flowed from a lustful heart, which led to adultery and, ultimately, to murder.

When does looking become lusting? It is all a matter of the condition of the heart. As Jesus said, "For out of the heart come evil thoughts, murder, adultery, sexual immorality, theft, false testimony, slander" (Matt. 15:19). The heart informs the mind how to interpret what was seen through the eyes. The heart that is pure appreciates the beauty of the opposite sex but does not long to possess what does not belong to it. The heart that is sexually immoral looks at the beauty of the opposite sex with selfish pleasure, for what it can gain. In the purity ministry for men this type of looking is called "snacking on a woman's beauty." It is selfishly devouring the beauty of another. It is not based on the length of time spent in looking. It is based on the attitude of the heart. Lustful looking is bent on visual titillation. Lust is a sin that violates both the seventh and tenth commandments, "You shall not commit adultery" and "You shall not covet" (Exod. 20:14, 17). Lust is a character issue.

What is the difference between love and lust?

If that is what lust is, what is the difference between love and lust?

The primary word for love in the New Testament is ἀγάπη [*agapē*], which is used to describe both human and divine love. Vine notes that ἀγάπη describes Christian love that "is not an impulse from the feelings, it does not always run with the natural inclinations, nor does it spend itself only upon those for whom some affinity is discovered."[191] Positively, *agapē* is giving, sacrificial, and other-centered. This volitional, sacrificial love is in marked contrast to the self-centered lust described in Matthew 5:28. The contrast between love and lust is clear from Table 2 below.

Table 2

Love vs. Lust

CHARACTERISTICS	LOVE	LUST
Object	You, other-centered	Me, self-centered
Goal	Please you	Please me, gratify my desires/fantasies
Focus	Heart focused	Body focused, objectification
Rights	Doesn't press rights	Presses rights
Orientation	Person-oriented	Performance-oriented
Emotions	No guilt, no shame	Feels guilty, ashamed
Result	Spouse feels clean, loved	Spouse feels dirty, used
Intimacy	Intimacy experienced	False intimacy perpetuated

Lust must be mortified.

Most commentators agree that Jesus' words in Matthew 5:29–30 regarding gouging out one's eye or amputating one's hand are not literal exhortations to self-mutilation:

---

[191] W. E. Vine, *Vine's Expository Dictionary of Old and New Testament Words* (Old Tappan, NJ: Fleming H. Revell Co, 1981), p. 21.

If your right eye causes you to sin, gouge it out and throw

it away. It is better for you to lose one part of your body

than for your whole body to be thrown into hell. And if your

right hand causes you to sin, cut it off and throw it away. It

is better for you to lose one part of your body than for your

whole body to go into hell (Matt. 5:29–30).

As Wiersbe notes, "Obviously, our Lord is not talking about literal surgery; for this would not solve the problem in the heart."[192] Rather Jesus is warning us to deal severely and decisively with sexual sin. MacArthur notes, "The intent of these words is simply to call for dramatic severing of the sinful impulses in us which push us to evil action (cf. Matt. 18:8–9)."[193] Sexual sin is deadly and must be mortified through radical spiritual surgery. The motto of Every Man's Battle For Purity, the men's purity ministry, is "Live Pure or Die!" We have come to believe that it is imperative that we live in purity. To do otherwise is to die spiritually, relationally, emotionally, physically, maritally, etc.

How to Gain a Pure Marriage

There are no shortcuts to gaining a pure marriage. Just as with becoming a pure man or woman, for a defiled marriage to become pure, repentance, confession, and the healing of the Holy Spirit are required.

Couple Repentance and Confession

Each partner must individually and as a couple repent of their sinful sexual practices. They must be broken over their sinfulness and repent for

---

[192] Warren Wiersbe, *The Bible Exposition Commentary* (Wheaton, IL: Victor Books, 1989), p. 24.

[193] MacArthur, p. 304.

what they have done. Like the younger son in Luke 15, they need to come to their senses and do honest "self talk." They need to call their sinfulness for what it is, sin and an offense to God. This will naturally lead to confession to God and one another. They need to ask for each other's forgiveness and purpose to turn from their wicked ways (2 Chron. 7:14). We have discussed in a previous chapter how much of the past should be confessed. The answer is as much as the spouse desires to know. The goal is a "no secrets" marriage with nothing hidden from either spouse.

The Healing of the Holy Spirit

God heals the brokenhearted (Ps. 147:3, Isa. 61:1). When we are brokenhearted over our sin, the Holy Spirit of God will heal our heart and cause us to know His forgiveness in our spirit. Our sin is cleansed by the power of Christ's blood. The power of that cleansing is made real and personal by the Holy Spirit. He causes the individual and couple who are cleansed to experience the joy of forgiveness. They are no longer plagued by the guilt and shame of their past.

Profile of a Pure Marriage

The husband and wife who are walking in purity will have drawn clear boundaries that keep out the sinful and let in the life affirming. Their boundaries include a zero tolerance policy for pornography in any of its forms. They desire a pure home so they do a "porn hunt" and smash, trash, or burn all pornography they find. They monitor their television and computer viewing to avoid soft-core pornography. They have Covenant Eyes or Net Accountability software installed on their computer and they ask accountability questions of each other. They practice modesty in their dress (1 Pet. 3:3) and permit the other to have the final say on how they clothe their bodies (1 Cor. 7:4). They are careful regarding the entertainment they permit themselves, avoiding anything that defiles whether in film, theater, or music. They are done with living as unbelievers live and no longer delight in the sinfulness of their past lifestyle (1 Pet. 4:3).

They delight to live in purity and in the stability of a loving, committed marriage. They have set clear boundaries around their relationships with the opposite sex. Like Joseph in the book of Genesis, they avoid compromising situations and when necessary flee. Finally, because love is the basis for their sexual intimacy, neither spouse in a pure marriage asks the other to do anything sexually that would make their partner feel uncomfortable, dirty, or used.

The benefit of all this is a marriage that reflects Christ and His Church. It is a marriage that is marked by intimacy, stability, faithfulness, and trust. The glory of Christ is seen in each partner and each views the other as God's gift to them.

Conclusion

The Bible's consistent message is that God's people are to live lives of holiness and purity. We are his image-bearers; how could we do less? The purity ministry is a radical call to recover the image of God in every man. It is a call to live in holiness. It is a ministry whose goals are sexual self-control for singles and sexual exclusivity and faithfulness for marrieds.

Marriage is a gift from God. It is designed both for the welfare and happiness of mankind to manifest His glory to a lost and darkened world. God meant marriage to be the permanent union of a heterosexual, monogamous couple in a covenant relationship with one another and Him that results in mutual joy and satisfaction.

CHAPTER NINE
THE POWER OF A PURE FAMILY

At Caesarea there was a man named Cornelius, a centurion in what was known as the Italian Regiment. He and all his family were devout and God-fearing ...

Acts 10:1–2

The Definition of Family

Probably one of the more divisive questions in sociological circles today is the definition of what constitutes a family. Is a family composed of a father, mother, and children? What about friends who live together for an extended period? Are they a family? The dictionary has a difficult time narrowing the definition of a family. The American College Dictionary says it is, "(a) parents and their children, whether dwelling together or not; (b) one's children collectively; (c) any group of persons closely related by blood, as parents, children, uncles, aunts, and cousins."[194] The online Merriam-Webster's Dictionary defines family as, "a group of individuals living under

---

[194] C. L. Barnhart (Ed.), *American College Dictionary.* New York, NY: Random House, 1960), pp. 435-436 .

one roof and usually under one head."[195] That definition has now replaced the more traditional Merriam-Webster's Dictionary definition of bygone years which said a family was, "the basic unit in society traditionally consisting of two parents rearing their children."

How does the Bible define a family? If we would define a family from the biblical perspective, we need to examine the first family created, Adam and Eve. Were Adam and Eve a family? Yes. A family need not have children to be a family. Adam and Eve, prior to the birth of Cain and Abel, were a family. Children, such as Cain, Abel, and later, Seth, merely expand the family. What about adoption? Are adopted children members of a family? As Christian believers, we are adopted into the family of God (Eph. 1:5). God makes provision for children to be adopted into a family. Therefore a biblical definition for family would be "any group of two or more people related by marriage, birth, or adoption" (cf.1 Tim. 5:8). As a working definition, I am using the term family to mean a nuclear family. Thus I am defining a family as one father, one mother, and one or more children whether by blood or adoption.

Jesus Redefines Family

In the physical world, a nuclear family is defined as one related by marriage, blood or adoption. Jesus, however, redefines the nuclear family by describing it as one related by faith in Him. Listen to His words to His disciples at the encounter with His mother and brothers:

> While Jesus was still talking to the crowd, his mother and
>
> brothers stood outside, wanting to speak to him. Someone
>
> told him, "Your mother and brothers are standing outside,

---

[195] *Family*, In *Merriam-Webster online dictionary* (Retrieved July 21, 2008, from http://www.merriam-webster.com/dictionary/family, 2008).

wanting to speak to you."

He replied to him, "Who is my mother, and who are my

brothers?" Pointing to his disciples, he said, "Here are

my mother and my brothers. For whoever does the will of

my Father in heaven is my brother and sister and mother"

(Matt. 12:46–50).

Jesus redefines family in light of the kingdom of God. In the kingdom, earthly relationships cease and spiritual relationships take on special significance (Matt. 22:30). It is those who do the will of God who are spiritual family. Commenting on Matthew 12:46–50, Tasker says of those who followed the Lord, "…there were some who responded to Jesus and in so doing showed that they were brought into so close a relationship with Himself that they could be said to constitute His family."[196]

Since there is no procreation of children in heaven, marriage is no longer needed. Heaven is populated, not through reproduction, but through salvation. Marriage, therefore, is clearly an earthbound relationship.

The Structure of the Family

The Foundation of Marriage

Families were designed by God to have order and structure. God's design is for families to be built on marriages. Marriage is the underlying foundation for the family structure. So before we can talk about the structure of the family, we must address the structure of marriage. According to Genesis 2:22–25, marriage was designed by God to be heterosexual ("woman…man"

---

[196] R. V. G. Tasker, "The Gospel According to St. Matthew, " In R. V. G. Tasker (Ed.),*Tyndale New Testament Commentaries* (Grand Rapids, MI: William B. Eerdmans Publishing Co., 1976), p. 133.

v. 22), monogamous ("a man...a woman" v. 24), exclusive ("leave his father and his mother" v. 24), permanent ("cleave to his wife" v. 24), progressively bonding ("shall become one flesh" v. 24), and sexual ("one flesh" v. 24). Marriage was always meant to be a relationship lived in the presence of God. In Genesis 3:8 it appears that, prior to the fall, it was common for Adam and Eve to walk with God among the trees of the garden. After the fall, they became afraid and hid from Him as He sought them out for their regular walk together.

The Roles of Family Members

From Genesis we see God's design for the husband. His roles in the family are to function as a father (Gen. 1:28), a provider (Gen. 2:15, 3:17–19) and a head (Gen. 3:16). The woman's roles are to function as a mother (Gen. 1:28), a helper (Gen. 2:18), and a submitter (Gen. 3:16). As we have seen in previous chapters, a husband bears responsibilities of leading, loving, sacrificing, sanctifying, providing, and protecting his family. God's design for a mother is also seen in Genesis. She bears the responsibilities of being an intimate companion, a conspicuous complement, a mother, and a joyful submitter to her husband. Together husband and wife are to love and nurture their children. Fathers are singled out to raise their children in the discipline and instruction of the Lord (Eph. 6:4).

Fathers are not to provoke their children.

Fathers are not to provoke their children to anger (Eph. 6:4 NASV). How does a father provoke his children to anger? The New International Version translates this phrase as "don't exasperate your children." What does it mean to *exasperate* your children and how do fathers do that to them? The word *exasperate* in the original language is the word παροργιζω [*parorgizo*], a compound word meaning, "to enrage, infuriate, or provoke to anger."[197] How do fathers infuriate and enrage their children? Here are four things fathers do which provoke that kind of response from their children:

(a) He breaks his promises. When a father opens his mouth and makes a promise to his sons or daughters, they take him seriously and expect him to keep his word. When a father breaks his word and does not fulfill the promise he made, his children lose faith in him, lose trust in him, and become infuriated inside. A godly father will keep his promises to his children no matter what! This is not a matter of convenience but of character. Broken promises are a form of lying. Is a man's word his bond or is it simply hot air? God keeps His promises to us (Num. 23:19, Josh. 23:14, Ps. 145:13) and expects us to keep our promises to one another (Eph. 4:25, Col. 3:9).

(b) He behaves hypocritically. Children readily spot hypocrisy. They know when a father is playing the "do as I say, not as I do" game. Children hear what a father says, but if it does not match what he does, children invariably believe what he does. For example, if father proclaims the importance of prayer but the children never see him pray, they conclude that prayer really isn't that important to him, nor will it be to them. Fathers also practice hypocrisy when they show two faces to their children: a public face that is one way and a private face that is quite the opposite. That kind of duplicity infuriates children. Jesus was particularly infuriated by the hypocrisy of the Pharisees who said one thing but did another (Matt. 23:28, Mark 12:15, Luke 12:1). Godly fathers are the same man in private as in public. The apostle Peter exhorts Christians to rid themselves of hypocrisy (1 Pet. 2:1).

---

[197] James Strong, "Greek Dictionary of the New Testament," *Strong's Exhaustive Concordance of the Bible,* p. 56

(c) He mistreats their mother. When a man disrespects, abuses, or becomes violent with his wife, his children become fearful and angry. They hear her cries. They hear the shouting and arguing. They see her bruises. Father becomes someone to be feared, someone who is a bully. What angers them is seeing their father who is stronger abusing their mother who is weaker. It is unfair and unjust. They want to defend her and stop the fighting. In addition, father and mother who should be the foundation and security for the family are not. That strikes terror into the heart of a child. Paul tells husbands, "... love your wives and do not be harsh with them" (Col. 3:19). When a man mistreats the mother of his children, he loses the respect of his children.

(d) He is absent without leave (AWOL). When a father is not there, his children become frustrated and lose heart (Col. 3:21). Whether through divorce, misplaced priorities, or emotional coldness, fathers who aren't physically and/or emotionally there for their children provoke them. If a father is absent, who will teach his children how a man thinks, feels, and behaves? Who will affirm them and validate them as worthwhile and important people? Who will love them and make them feel wanted? Mother cannot make up for father's absence. He is AWOL and the family will suffer for it. Fathers can be there physically, but be emotionally absent. Emotionally absent fathers do not express their feelings for their children. Their children never hear that they are loved, wanted, important, valuable, and good at something. This leaves children frustrated and angry about what they didn't get but needed in the form of emotional support. All of these are ways in which a father can provoke his children.

Children are to obey their parents in the Lord.

Children, on the other hand, are to obey their parents in the Lord

(Eph. 6:1–2).[198] Children are not called to set the standards for the family. They are called to obey the standards established by their parents for the family. The ideal is for parents who love Jesus Christ to love one another. Together, parents are to love their children. When this type of family relationship occurs, children can rest in the security of their parents' love.

The Ministries of a Family

We have described the structure of a family but we still need to answer why God made families in the first place. What are they supposed to do? According to the Bible, God put families on the earth for a number of reasons:

(a) To fulfill His command to "be fruitful and increase in number and fill the earth" (Gen. 1:28). Thus a family is God's context for bearing and raising children.

(b) To fulfill God's command to "subdue it (the earth)" (Gen. 1:28). A second function of a family is to subdue the earth or tame it through work. Individual members invest in their family through working for the good of the family. As Solomon writes, "Two are better than one, because they have a good return for their work" (Ecclesiastes 4:9). Thus, work is not a curse. It is a blessing.

(c) To reflect Christ to the world. The final function of a family is to bear both a personal and a corporate witness to Jesus Christ. Let's look at each

---

[198] What does Paul mean by "obey your parents in the Lord?" Here are several possible explanations: (a) children are to obey Christian parents only, those who are "in Christ." Does this mean that children do not have to obey non-Christian parents? Hardly. (b) Children are to obey their parents because they, the children, are Christians ("in the Lord") and such obedience honors their parents. (c) Children are to obey their parents as an act of worship unto the Lord. Explanation (b) seems to be the closest to the apostle Paul's intention.

ministry.

The Ministry of Fruit Bearing

Families, like all living entities, are to bear fruit. One of the primary functions of a family is to bear children. Reproduction is the means for growing the human race. It is the way one generation replaces the next. In the Old Testament, children were considered a blessing of the Lord; the family with many were wealthy indeed (Ps. 127:3–5, 1 Sam. 1:8). The family is the best environment for raising children. Within the safety and structure of a healthy family, children can model themselves after mother and father, learn social and occupational skills, gain a positive self-image, and be loved and nurtured.

Why do some couples not want children? The primary reason is fear. They may be afraid to have children because they are not sure they will be competent parents. They may be afraid they will repeat the dysfunctionality of their family-of-origin. They may be afraid to give birth or afraid to grow up and become adults. They may be afraid of bringing children into a world as dangerous and corrupt as ours. They may be afraid they cannot afford children. "After all," they reason, "we can barely pay our own expenses. How could we ever pay for a baby?" Whatever the reason, fear is holding them back from obeying God's command to be fruitful.

Some couples are selfish and do not want children because children would interfere with their lifestyles or careers. Finally, there are couples who do not want children because their marital relationship is conflictual. They reason that it would be damaging to bring a child into such a marriage.

The Ministry of Work

Families were designed to work together. Why did families in the Old

Testament want many children? In an agrarian society many children provided many hands to help with the chores. Jacob was a wealthy man having twelve sons to tend his flocks and herds.[199] Work preceded the Fall (Gen. 2:15) and reflects God who worked in creation (Gen. 2:2). It is quite common for families to work in a family business or enterprise. Not only does this provide income for the family and a trade for the children, but it also provides a legacy for the future. Future generations will preserve the family business and keep it going.

For Christian families, serving together in ministry is a wonderful experience. Whether it is a musical ministry, a ministry to the poor, or a ministry to children, working together promotes unity and other-centeredness. It teaches children that the family doesn't exist just for itself. It exists to serve the Lord (Eph. 2:10).

Reflect Christ to the World

The final function of a family is to bear both a personal and a corporate witness to Jesus Christ. How does a family do that? Before answering that question, let's first be clear that we are called personally and corporately to be witnesses for Christ. Jesus told His disciples that the Holy Spirit would empower them to be His witnesses to all the world (Acts 1:8). As the apostle Paul declares, "we are therefore Christ's ambassadors…" (2 Cor. 5:20). Being a witness for Christ is non-optional for believers. The lost need to be saved and the only way that will happen is if we, who believe in Jesus Christ, bear witness to Him and His power in our lives (Rom. 10:14–17).

Family members, then, bear personal witness by sharing the good

---

[199] Similarly, Jesus Christ was spiritually wealthy having twelve disciples to carry on the spiritual work of spreading the gospel (cf. Matt. 10:1, Matt 28:18–20).

news of Jesus Christ with those who are lost and need the Savior. Through building relationships with the lost, God opens doors of opportunity to share the gospel. Believers are to live grace-filled lives so that their lives and their lips are consistent.

As a unit, the family also has a corporate witness. It reflects Christ to their community. Neighbors need to see a difference in how they live and hear from their lips how Christ makes that difference in their family. It is too easy for Christians to be silent in their verbal witness such that their neighbors never know they are Christians. Without a verbal witness, neighbors could assume that the family is moral but not necessarily Christians.

How does a family reflect Christ? One of the clearest ways is how they handle crisis and tragedy. Families who reflect Christ truly trust Him in the midst of the crisis. They pray fervently and press into God. They hang onto the promises of God and they believe that God does work all things for good for those who trust Him. When tragedy hits they refuse to take the path of Job's wife, i.e. "curse God and die" (Job 2:8).

A second way a family reflects Christ is they prioritize attending church together. In a post-Christian world which treats Sunday as any other day to work or play, assembling with other Christians on Sundays becomes a powerful witness. Acts 2:42–47 describes the powerful impact of the church in Jerusalem. When the church assembles today, the same four functions take place. It is in church that the family is strengthened in its walk with Christ through teaching. It is in church that the family fellowships with like-minded believers in Jesus Christ. It is in church that the family combines forces with others to meet needs that could not be met privately. It is in church that the combined prayers of the saints ascend to the throne of God (cf. Rev. 8:4).

The Attack on the Purity of the Family

Like marriage, the family is under attack today. Just as marriage was God's idea and therefore hated by Satan, so families are God's idea and equally hated by the evil one. The devil is attacking the family as never before, so much so that the family, as we have known it, is rapidly disappearing. If it does disappear, what will take its place? Gene Veith writes:

> The dissolution of the family as the basic unit of society means that all of its authority, powers, and responsibilities go, instead, to the government. The state is increasingly assuming the role of the father, functions as the provider, the protector, and the disciplinarian. The state is also assuming the role of the mother, concerned about our health, nagging us about eating right and avoiding bad habits, and forcing us to be sensitive, well-mannered, and nice.[200]

Why is the family disappearing? What is Satan's strategy to destroy the family? It is a three-fold attack.

The Attack on the Heart of the Family

Satan's strategy begins with an attack on the heart of the family, marriage. God's design for the family since the creation of Adam and Eve has centered on marriage. A family is built upon one husband married to one wife with one or more children. That simple structure is under attack as never before. According to the 2004 census of the U.S. Census Bureau, 58.4 percent of children under 18 years of age lived with both biological parents

---

[200] Gene E. Veith, "Uncommon Bond: Family Collapse Opens a Door for Totalitarianism," *World*, July 12/19, 2008, *23,* 29.

who were married to one another.[201] That is down from 85 percent in 1970.[202] To what do we attribute this decline? A lenient, "no-fault" divorce law is one of the primary offenders. Divorce is not a new concept. Couples have been divorcing since the days of the Old Testament. God gave laws to His people, Israel, to regulate divorce (Deut. 22:19, 29; 24:1–4). Jesus reaffirmed those laws in the New Testament (Matt. 5:31–32; 19:1–9). Divorce is not new but the ease of obtaining one is. Easy divorce laws in the United States have wreaked havoc by providing a "quick solution" to a painful relationship. This has exponentially escalated the number of couples divorcing and in so doing has destabilized the family. Couples who would have stayed together in past generations now end in divorce. In a former generation marriages survived because couples honored their wedding vows or for the sake of the children. That is no longer the case. Couples routinely go back on their vows and no longer consider their children ahead of themselves. Unfortunately, children pay the price for this kind of selfish sinfulness. Nearly every study done on the impact of divorce on children indicates that it has a negative effect.[203] The

---

[201] Robert Bernstein, "Majority of Children Live with Two Biological Parents," posted February 20, 2008 (*U. S. Census Bureau News,* Retrieved August 3, 2008, from http://www.census.gov/PressRelease/www/releases/archives/children/011507.html).

[202] Sam Roberts, "Most Children Still Live in Two-Parent Homes, Census Bureau Reports," posted February 21, 2008 (*The New York Times,* Retrieved August 3, 2008 from http://www.nytimes.com/2008/02/21/us/21census.html).

[203] Sara McLanahan and Gary Sandefur, *Growing Up with a Single Parent: What Hurts, What Helps,* (Cambridge: Harvard University Press, 1994), p. 19. Also a well-written summary of the detrimental effects of divorce on children can be found on the Focus on the Family website: http://www.family.org/socialissues/A000001127.cfm. It is written by Glenn Stanton and is entitled, "Why Marriage Matters for Children: Children with Married Parents Consistently Do Better than Their Peers who Have Single, Cohabiting, Divorced or Step-Parents."

devil is attacking the heart of the family, marriage.

The Attack on Roles in the Family

The roles of men prior to 1960 were clearly understood. Men worked outside the home to provide income for the family. Women worked in the home to care for the home and children. Feminism turned those roles on their heads. Women began entering the workforce in record numbers in the 1970s. But if both parents work full time in the marketplace, who cares for the children? In a best-case scenario, the answer is both parents worked out their schedules to accommodate parenting their children. Many entrusted their children to others to parent such as daycare centers, grandparents, nannies, or preschools. Some had no answer and a generation of "latch key" kids was born. Latch key kids let themselves into their homes and were left alone until their parents arrived home from work. This was not a good solution. All of these solutions resulted in pushing parenting into a place of secondary importance behind providing. Once again children were the casualties.

Then there is the confusion over who is head of the family. Since both parents share equally in providing income for the family, caring for the children, performing chores around the house, and seem to be equal in every way, why should the husband be considered the head of the family and why must the wife submit to him? Accordingly, many families have abandoned the biblical roles of husband as head of the family and wife as submitter to the husband. Many have now drifted into an equal (egalitarian or equalitarian) approach to family leadership with no one as the head and no one as the submitter. This sounds reasonable at first blush but it produces internal chaos in the home, defective role models for children, and flies in the face of the clear teaching of the Bible. The equal or egalitarian approach to family leadership often results in a passive husband and a usurping wife.[204]

The Attack on the Purity of the Family

The third wave of attack against the family is the onslaught of sexual immorality. Men are called by God to be the heads or leaders of their families (1 Cor. 11:3, Eph. 5:23). Piper and Grudem explain, "In the home, biblical headship is the husband's divine calling to take primary responsibility for Christlike leadership, protection, and provision."[205] The devil understands that and attacks the family by attacking the purity of the head of the family, the husband. He rightly understands that if husbands can be corrupted by sexual sin they cannot lead their families into holiness. How can sexually impure husbands lead their families to become virtuous and moral? How can husbands set the standard for morality and spirituality if they are living hypocritical, duplicitous lives? Of even greater significance, how can men, the image-bearers of God, reflect His holiness if they are living in sexual unholiness? They cannot. The devil knows this and relentlessly attacks men with sexual temptations. This is not to minimize the sexual attack on wives, but Satan knows wives were not appointed by God to be the head of the family. He attacks the husband believing that if he can defile the head of the

---

[204] Wayne Grudem, *Evangelical Feminism and Biblical Truth,* p. 43. As Grudem says, "I believe that an egalitarian position, with its constant blurring of the distinctions between men and women, will lead to a gender identity crisis in men and women, and especially in many of the children that they raise. Men and women will be confused about what it means to be a man and what it means to be a woman, and how men and women should act in ways that are different from one another ... As a result, I believe that the egalitarian position will lead to an increasing breakdown of families and a weakening and effeminization of the church," p. 532.

[205] John Piper and Wayne Grudem, *50 Crucial Questions: An Overview of Central Concerns about Manhood and Womanhood.* Adapted from *Recovering Biblical Manhood and Womanhood* (Wheaton, IL: Crossway Books, 1992), p. 16.

family he can cripple the family.

How a Family Becomes Pure

The Porn Hunt

Family purity begins with parental purity and flows outward to the children. We have already seen in previous chapters how a man and woman become pure. Together a pure husband and wife establish a pure, undefiled environment for their children. This means that they purify their home of everything defiling. In the purity ministry we call this a "porn hunt." In a porn hunt, parents scour their home for pornography or anything morally or spiritually defiling.

> **"Family purity begins with parental purity and flows outward to the children"**

All pornography, regardless of the form it takes, is removed from the house and burned or destroyed. A porn hunt will also include sanitizing computers, televisions, cell phones, personal digital assistants (PDAs), and any other vehicles for pornography to insure that they are safe and filtered. Hard drives on electronic equipment defiled by pornography must be cleansed or replaced. Accountability software and internet filters must be installed.

Family Standards for Purity

A pure environment will also mean family standards for privacy are established so family members can feel safe to dress and bathe in privacy. It will also include family standards for dress and attire both inside and outside of the house. Inside the home, family members should be encouraged to wear clothing or robes rather than underwear or nudity. Modesty and discretion are the rule for all dress. Family purity will also include purity of speech. Family members need to be taught to speak about sexuality in modest terms and to not make light or joke about the subject. Finally, outside of the home family members must dress modestly so as not to draw attention to themselves sexually. Children must not frequent the homes of friends with different moral standards or who have unprotected, unsafe computers. To do so is to invite trouble. The biblical principle is that, "Bad company corrupts good character," (1 Cor. 15:33). Our responsibility is to safeguard our children against wickedness in our world.

Parental Teaching on Healthy Sexuality

Parents need to teach their children about healthy sexuality. It is their privilege and responsibility as parents. Their teaching will involve talking to their children about sexuality in age-appropriate ways. It is wise for parents to talk to their children together as a team. As Mark Laaser says:

> When we talk to our children about sex, we must strive
> to teach them a positive perspective about it, one that
> celebrates sex as a part of the God-ordained relationship
> between a husband and wife... The main dynamic we
> demonstrate by (talking as a team to our children) is that a
> man and woman can talk together about this subject.[206]

In a pure family, father and mother understand what constitutes incest and how to guard against it. They will teach their children about safe touch versus unsafe touch. They will teach their children about what safe touch is and who can/should touch them. They will teach them what to do if someone attempts to touch them inappropriately. At the appropriate age (typically pre-teen), father and mother will teach their children about the value of virginity

---

[206] Mark Laaser, *Talking to Your Kids about Sex: How to Have a Lifetime of Age-Appropriate Conversations with Your Children about Healthy Sexuality* (Colorado Springs, CO: WaterBrook Press, 1999), pp. 35, 66.

and why it is God's standard and theirs as a family. They will teach them how to respond to those who don't hold to this same standard and who want them to compromise themselves sexually.

Parents must teach their children about making wise choices when encountering sexuality in the media. They will talk with them about boundaries for television, computer, cell phone, and other electronic media. All family members will honor the family rules—parents and children. They will address the issue of how to handle unacceptable television programs, movies, computer games, or websites when visiting friends. They will teach their children what to say to those friends whose families have a different standard for purity.

Intergenerational Family Purity

In Genesis 1, Moses writes that all living creatures reproduced "after their own kind" (Gen. 1:11, 21, 24). The biblical principle is clear. All living things reproduce after their own kind … dogs reproduce dogs not cats. What is true in the physical realm is equally true in the moral and spiritual realms. Pure families reproduce pure families. Intergenerational purity is not an accident. Pure families do not just happen. They are the result of good parenting. They are the result of intentional effort and training by pure parents and grandparents.

In an impure world, pure families stand out like stars in the dark night sky (cf. Phil. 2:15). Christians must do all within their power to protect themselves and their families from the contamination of the world.

The Benefits of Purity to a Family

Why should a family live in purity? The cost of swimming against the tide in a culture drowning in immorality is high, so why do it? Here are four reasons. The first is because it pleases God. Purity is God's will for families and living in purity pleases Him (Eph. 5:8–10). Families exist to glorify God and the best way they can glorify Him is to love Him and live as He commands. He commands purity (1 Pet. 1:16).

A second reason for living in purity is that it is the type of life God blesses. God calls the pure life the righteous life. To live a righteous, moral life is the highest standard of living possible. God hates sin and loves righteousness; therefore, He blesses the family living in righteousness with His presence, His protection, and His power (Ps. 5:12; 146:8).

A third reason to be pure as a family is to be a witness to the lost. As mentioned earlier, Christian families are to be a corporate witness to the lost. Purity enables them to do this. If a Christian family lives no differently than the lost, what is the difference Christ Jesus makes in a family? There is none. Purity is also a corporate witness and encouragement to the saved. Pure families in the church encourage each other to live in purity (cf. Heb. 3:13).

Finally, a pure family is protected against the fallout of sexual immorality in the world: sexually-transmitted diseases, unwanted pregnancies, guilt, and the emotional repercussions of sexual sin.

CHAPTER TEN
CONCLUSION

If we confess our sins, he is faithful and just and will forgive us our sins and purify us from all unrighteousness.

1 John 1:9

This book has been about the power of purity. Who is the power source for purity? God. God provides the power and motivation to live a pure life. God, the Holy Spirit, is a holy—not an unholy—spirit. He resides within every believer in Jesus Christ convicting them of sin, righteousness, and judgment to come. He provides the power to live a pure life.

The power of purity is about God's power but it is also about the power of a pure man, a pure woman, a pure marriage, and a pure family. When a man or woman is living in purity, they have a powerful life. They are powerful witnesses to the difference Christ makes in lives. They are powerful examples to their children, family, friends, co-workers, and neighbors. They reap the harvest of righteousness in their personal lives. The pure man or woman has a powerful prayer life, powerful ministry, and powerful worship. God honors and blesses purity. God disciplines and chastises impurity.

A question that is often asked is, "Why are Christians so vulnerable to sexual impurity?" Have we dropped our guard in this area and been deceived by the evil one? Have we grown lazy or indifferent to God's command to be holy? Have we simply settled for a lower standard of purity? Are pastors not preaching about sexual sin and warning their flocks? All these reasons are often cited but let's consider one reason seldom considered—the cost of personal sacrifice. The Bible calls us to sacrifice our lives (Luke 9:23–24; Rom. 12:1–2). With any sacrifice, a price must be paid. In the Old Testament, when a man or woman sacrificed a lamb, they paid a price. That lamb could have been sold for money or it could have been butchered to supply food for the family. Either way it costs the sacrificer something. Sacrifice is never easy and never cheap. It is never convenient.

Convenience Christianity and the Call to Sacrifice

We live in a culture of convenience. We don't like to be inconvenienced ever for anything any time. Whether it's the convenience of getting our morning coffee from Starbucks via the drive-through lane so we don't have to park and go inside, to refusing to wait in line to be seated in a restaurant, we don't like to be inconvenienced. Churches, like the rest of society, cater to our demand for convenience as well. In the summertime people like to use their weekends to go to their cabins or on vacation and it's inconvenient for them to go to church, so we cancel or scale back worship services. Convenience thinking pushes leaders to want everything to be easy for their people: easy worship, easy Bible study, easy ministry, easy Christianity.

This is especially seen in how the church ministers to men.

"Don't expect too much from men," "Make it convenient for

men because we can't ask too much from them" These are the mottos of Convenience Christianity. This raises the question, "When are men ever taught to sacrifice for a cause greater than the accumulation of money and things?" "When are men ever taught to sacrifice for something greater than themselves?"

Convenience is the enemy of sacrifice! It was not convenient for Jesus to die on the cross. It was a sacrifice. Writing of Jesus, the author of Hebrews declares, "because by one *sacrifice* he has made perfect forever those who are being made holy" (Heb. 10:14, emphasis mine). Had He wanted the convenient life, Jesus would have listened to the devil, bowed down to him, and avoided the cross completely (Matt. 4:9). Had He wanted the convenient life, Jesus would never have come to earth in the first place. The devil loves Convenience Christianity but hates sacrifice!

We cannot be holy and pure without sacrifice. It will never be convenient to live a life of purity. It will always be a sacrifice. In the purity ministry, men arrive at Purity Boot Camp at 6:00 a.m. Why so early? Because men do not need Purity Boot Camp to be convenient for them. Men need to sacrifice some sleep and pay a price for their purity. Why is it required of men that they hold one another accountable daily in the Purity Platoons? Men need to sacrifice their isolation and lack of accountability. Men need to do the hard thing! Sacrifice builds character. Sacrifice produces spiritual depth and maturity. Sacrifice makes the prize valuable. Convenience is the enemy of sacrifice and the enemy of purity!

The Divine Partnership

God is calling us to sacrifice convenience and enter into a "divine partnership" with Him for the cause of purity. What does it mean to "partner with God?" There is a work in becoming pure which only God can perform and there is a work which God requires us to perform—one which He will not perform. On God's side of the equation, only God can purify the heart of a sinner. Only God can make the unclean clean, the impure pure. He alone can change a heart. "Heart" is not referring to the physical organ which pumps blood through the body. Rather heart, as used in the Bible, means the core or essence of a person. Your heart is the core of your being. Your heart is where your values and beliefs are stored (Rom. 10:9–10). Your heart is the seat of your affections (1 Tim. 5:1). Purity starts in the heart (Ps. 24:3–4; 51:10; 73:1). Only God can change a heart. Our hearts are "deceitful and wicked;" we can't even know them (Jer. 17:9). So that's God's divine work, not ours. Purity starts with God performing a miraculous heart transplant. He replaces my sinful heart, with its sinful values and desires, with a holy heart that desires righteousness and purity.

On our side of the equation is the work of purifying our lives of all that is ungodly, impure, and unclean. We are required to carry out the box of porn magazines from the basement and burn it. We are required to install accountability software on our computers. We are required to make a covenant with our eyes "not to look lustfully upon a young woman" (Job 31:1). All of those and many more are required of us as we discipline ourselves and raise the standard of holiness in our lives. The apostle Paul writes, "Since we have these promises, dear friends, let us purify ourselves from everything that contaminates body and spirit, perfecting holiness out of reverence for God" (2 Cor. 7:1). God has chosen to place the responsibility for disciplining ourselves to become more holy on us. God commands us to be holy saying, "Be holy, because I am holy" (1 Pet. 1:16). He could do all the practical work of holiness if He wanted to. He could make the box of porn magazines disappear. He could override our wills and make us desire to live pure lives. He could strike us blind every time we looked with lust upon a woman (Matt. 5:28). He could—but He doesn't. Rather, He has chosen to partner with us in this great calling of sanctification.

In a lot of ways, the divine partnership for purity is similar to the divine partnership for evangelism. Who can save someone? Only God. Only God can take a lost, hell-bound sinner and save him because only God can change a heart. Transformation of sinners into saints is God's job. Who is commanded to preach the good news of salvation in Jesus Christ alone? Who are to be His witnesses? We are. God has given us the sublime privilege and responsibility of proclaiming the life-transforming, destiny-changing gospel to the lost. He could do it but He's chosen to use us as His ambassadors. That's an amazing partnership!

The purpose of a purity ministry is to call men and women to purity so that God can transform their hearts. We then give them the tools they need to discipline their lives. Purity is a divine partnership. Both halves of the equation are essential for us to live holy lives.

Establishing a Purity Ministry

This book has been about the power of purity. It has not addressed how, in practical terms, to establish a purity ministry in a local church. That is the subject of the next book, *The Purity of the Bride*. In *The Purity of the Bride* many questions are addressed such as: "What does a purity ministry look like in a local church? What is required to launch it? How is the resistance to the sensitivity of the subject overcome in a local church? What resources are available?" Everything from curriculum, to budgeting, to sample policies for church boards, to personnel required, to leadership training is addressed in the book.

The vision of the National Coalition For Purity (NCFP) is "to purify the Bride of Christ, one church at a time." There are no shortcuts and no easy answers. Purifying the Bride of Christ requires the power of God. It will not happen without Him. The mission of NCFP is "to challenge, resource, and train every church in America in sexual purity." That is the reason for writing the next book, *The Purity of the Bride*. It is meant to be a tool to equip the Bride to be pure. Finally, the purpose of NCFP is "to make sexual purity an unavoidable issue for the Church of Jesus Christ." Purity is my passion and prayer for the church. May it be yours as well!

TWELVE REASONS WHY MASTURBATION IS NOT GOD'S WILL

Here are twelve biblical principles impacting masturbation:

1. It is rooted in lust. Masturbation is a behavior rooted in lustful thinking. Men and women don't masturbate in a vacuum. All masturbators are thinking about something. Typically, masturbators are visualizing either pornography viewed in the past or real or imagined sexual encounters with women or men. The Bible consistently condemns all lust and lustful thinking as sinful (Matt. 5:27–28; Rom. 1:24).

2. Our bodies don't belong to us. Our bodies don't belong to us to do with as we please. Our bodies were bought by the Lord Jesus Christ and belong to Him and, if married, to our husbands or wives (1 Cor. 7:4).

3. It is either adultery or fornication. Adultery is defined as having sex with someone other than one's spouse while married. Fornication is sex between unmarried people. Masturbation is self-sex. Because the masturbator is having sex with him- or herself rather than his or her spouse, he or she is committing adultery with him- or herself. All forms of adultery and fornication are sinful (Heb. 13:4).

4. It renders men morally unclean. Masturbation involves the discharge of seminal fluid. From the Mosaic Law, to discharge semen is to render oneself unclean before God and unfit for worship (Lev. 15:16).

Although the New Testament says we are spiritually clean in Christ, the New Testament never negates any Old Testament moral law. Rather Christ affirms the moral law and even clarifies its original intent (Matt. 5:17–20).

5. Sex was designed to bond husbands and wives. The biblical teaching is that all sexual intercourse (including any emission of semen) is to be between a husband and wife within the committed relationship of marriage. Sex bonds husbands and wives (Heb. 13:4, 1 Cor. 7:3). Every instance of healthy, godly sexuality mentioned in the Bible is in the context of a heterosexual, covenant marriage relationship. All sexual energy is to be directed toward one's spouse in the context of a covenant marriage.

6. It defrauds a spouse of that which belongs to him or her. As a man or woman continuously masturbates, they defraud their spouse of their body and the sexual relationship that belongs to him or her (1 Cor. 7:3–5). Addiction research has shown that constant masturbation desensitizes a person to physical intercourse.

7. It is lack of self-control. God commends self-control for both singles and marrieds. He warns marrieds to engage in sexual relations with their spouses because of their lack of self-control (Gal. 5:23, 1 Cor. 7:5). Masturbation by singles or marrieds is self-sex, not self-control.

8. It deprives a person of holiness. Sanctification (holiness) involves abstaining from all sexual immorality. Masturbation, being sexual immorality and impurity, deprives us of sanctification (1 Thess. 4:3,7).

9. It produces false intimacy. Masturbation can never provide true intimacy with God or our spouse. It is an act of selfishness that only produces false intimacy (Gen. 2:24).

10. It is a sin against one's own body. Because masturbation is a form of sexual immorality and all sexual immorality is a sin against one's own body (1 Cor. 6:18), masturbation is a sin against one's own body.

11. It can become our master. Masturbation can become an addictive practice and gain mastery over us so that we cannot quit. We try to quit but fail repeatedly. We can find ourselves in bondage to this addictive behavior and it becomes our master (1 Cor. 6:12). Jesus Christ alone is to be our Master and Lord (Matt. 23:8, John 13:13, Eph. 6:9).

12. It involves secrecy and shame. Masturbation is done in private and in secret. It is shame producing to the masturbator. Anything that must be done in secret and produces shame is not the will of God. God intended sex to be a private practice, not a secretive practice, done within the sanctity of marriage. He never intended sex to be a shame-producing behavior (Gen. 2:25).[1]

---

[1] Irving A. Woolf, *Purity Platoon Battle Plans* (Maple Grove, MN: National Coalition For Purity, 2008), pp. 35-37.

AM I SEXUALLY ADDICTED?
ASSESSMENT

By Dr. Irv Woolf

To complete the assessment, answer each question by placing a check in the appropriate True/False column and total each column when completed.

True	False		
True	False	1.	I have few or no close male friendships
True	False	2.	I often have mood swings meaning I swing from excited to depressed quickly.
True	False	3	I am overly friendly with females.
True	False	4.	It is normal for me to do "alternative monitoring" (i.e. scanning the room/roaming eyes) for women, even in the company of my wife or girlfriend.
True	False	5.	I have no one holding me accountable in my personal life or at work.
True	False	6.	I have a poor attention span and tend to "zone out" or lose focus in conversations.
True	False	7.	I am demanding of sex.
True	False	8.	I spend a lot of unaccountable time on the computer.
True	False	9.	I am a "Type A" or driven personality.
True	False	10.	I have a decrease in my sex drive.
True	False	11.	I have issues with anger and frequently have anger outbursts (i.e. shouting, threats, rage).
True	False	12.	I have a loss of sleep or appetite.
True	False	13.	I isolate and am seen as a loner.
True	False	14.	I am a people-pleaser.
True	False	15.	I have trouble making eye contact with people.
True	False	16.	I change the topic of conversation to avoid discussing my vulnerability.
True	False	17.	I frequently lie and practice deception.
True	False	18.	I believe that sex equals intimacy.
True	False	19.	I abuse things such as food, work, alcohol, drugs, exercise, etc.
True	False	20.	I have to be in control of the finances in our home.
True	False	21.	I am controlling of my wife and children.
True	False	22.	I always have to have the last word.
True	False	23.	I am passive and usually in a relationship with a strong female.
True	False	24.	I struggle with fears of failure, rejection, and abandonment.
True	False	25.	I minimize, intellectualize, excuse, or deny my sexual sin.

Total TRUE answers_____   Total FALSE answers_____

THE COST OF IMPURITY

What would it cost you if you gave up your sexual purity?

I.   Personal Cost

II.   Marital Cost

III.   Family Cost

IV.   Church Cost

V.   Employment Cost

VI.   Friendship Cost

VII.   Opposite Sex Cost

VIII.   Spiritual Cost

IX.   Financial Cost

X.   Health Cost

XI.   Emotional Cost

GLOSSARY

Adultery sexual unfaithfulness, physically or emotionally, to one's spouse.

Fornication sexual intercourse between two unmarried people.

Free in the context of this book, describes a person who is no longer controlled by sexual sin. Freedom occurs when the Spirit of God transforms the heart of a person, breaks the chains of sexual bondage, and sets him or her free to walk in joyful purity. A person can be pure (sober) but not free. Freedom involves a changed heart. Purity involves a comfortably constrained flesh.

Grace can be defined as "God doing for us, in us, and through us what we cannot do for ourselves—through the person and power of Jesus Christ."[2]

Marriage is defined as the legal union of one man and one woman.

Marital commitment refers to dedication to the relationship's continuance.

Marital satisfaction is defined as the degree of contentment and gratification one feels toward the marriage relationship.

Pornography any visual, written, or recorded stimulus designed to cultivate or heighten a person's desire toward immoral sexual behavior. Thus, pornography would encompass sexually explicit chat, erotic stories, pictures, movies, virtual sex, etc.

Pure is understood to describe a person who has ceased from sexually acting out. In terms of the men's purity ministry, Every Man's Battle For Purity, pure describes a man who has ceased from masturbation, viewing pornography in any of its forms, and entertaining sexual fantasies for a period of six months. Only then would that man be considered pure. In the medical addiction model, pure would be the equivalent of "sober."

---

[2] Daniel Henderson, *Think Before You Look* (Chattanooga, TN: AMG Publishers, 2005), p. 19.

Purity ministry involves the focus of a local church or organization on sexual purity. It can be a broad approach addressing sexual purity at every age group from children to adults including both genders, or it can be narrowly focused on adult men over eighteen years of age.

Sex is understood to mean "any behavior producing arousal whose intent is orgasm."[3] The term "gender" is employed to refer to men or women and the term "sex" is limited to sexual behavior.

Sexual abuse is the wrongful use of sex which hurts or harms another, often as a means of control.

Sex addict is a non-pejorative term meaning an image-bearer of Almighty God who is enslaved to sexual sin and under its mastery.

Sexual addiction is "a pathological relationship with any form of sexual activity."[4] Sexual addiction is further defined as the inability to cease and desist from any sexual behavior. Biblical synonyms for addiction are "mastery," "slavery," and "bondage."

Sexual immorality encompasses any sexual behavior outside the boundaries of a husband and wife relationship within marriage. Sexual immorality is the English translation of the Greek term, πορνεία [*porneia*].

---

[3] Hyde and DeLamater, p. 3.
[4] Earle and Laaser, p. 12.

REFERENCES

Aland, K., Black, M., Martini, C., Metzger, B., & Wikgren, A. E. (Eds.). (1968). *Greek New Testament* (2nd ed.). Stuttgart, West Germany: Wurttemberg Bible Society.

Alcorn, R. C. (2000). *Restoring Sexual Sanity: Christians in the Wake of the Sexual Revolution*. Ft. Lauderdale, FL: Coral Ridge Ministries.

Allender, D. B., & Longman, T. I. (1995). *Intimate Allies*. Wheaton, IL: Tyndale House.

American Psychiatric Association. (1994). *Diagnostic and Statistical Manual of Mental Disorders* (4th ed.). Washington, DC: American Psychiatric Association.

American Psychological Association. (2001). *Publication Manual of the American Psychological Association* (5th ed.). Washington, DC: American Psychological Association.

Anderson, N.T. (2008). *Winning the Battle Within*. Eugene, OR: Harvest House Publishers.

Anderson, N. T. (1990). *The Bondage Breaker*. Eugene, OR: Harvest House Publishers.

Anderson, N.T. & Mylander, C. (2006). *Experiencing Christ Together*. Ventura, CA: Regal Books.

Anderson, N. T. & Saucy, R. L. (1997). *The Common Made Holy: Being Conformed to the Image of God.* Eugene, OR: Harvest House Publishers.

Anonymous. (1989). *Sexaholics Anonymous*. Simi Valley, CA: SA Literature.

Arndt, W. F., & Gingrich, F. W. (1971). *A Greek-English Lexicon of the New Testament and Other Early Christian Literature* (4th ed.). Chicago, IL: U of Chicago Press.

Arterburn, S., & Stoeker, F. (2000). *Every Man's Battle: Winning the War on Sexual Temptation One Victory at a Time*. Colorado Springs, CO: Waterbrook Press.

Barnhart, C. L. (Ed.). (1960). *American College Dictionary*. New York, NY: Random House.

Beck, J. R., & Demarest, B. (2005). *The Human Person in Theology and Psychology*. Grand Rapids, MI: Kregel Publications.

Bernstein, R. (2008, February 20). "Majority of Children Live with Two Biological Parents." *U.S. Census Bureau News*. Retrieved August 3, 2008, from http://www.census.gov/Press-Release/www/releases/archives/children/011507.html.

Black, J. S. (1995). "Pornography, Masturbation, and Other Private Misuses: A Perversion of Intimacy." *The Journal of Biblical Counseling , 13 (3)*, 7–10.

Brody, J. E. (2000, May 22). "Cybersex Leads to Psychological Disorder." *New York Times News Service*, 1–33.

Brown, F., Driver, S. R., & Briggs, C. A. (1972). *A Hebrew and English Lexicon of the Old Testament*. Oxford, England: The Clarendon Press.

Bull, L. (November 1, 2007). "American Youth Uninformed on Sexual Health." Retrieved July 7, 2008 from *RH Reality Check*: http://www.rhrealitycheck.org/blog/2007/11/01/american-youth-seriously-uninformed-   on-sexual-health.

Carnes, P. (1992). *Don't Call it Love: Recovery from Sexual Addiction*. New York, NY: Bantam Books.

Carnes, P. (2001). *Out of the Shadows: Understanding Sexual Addiction* (3rd ed.). Center City, MN: Hazelden.

Chafer, L. S. (1993). *Systematic Theology*. Grand Rapids, MI: Kregel Publications.

Cloud, H., & Townsend, J. (1999). *Boundaries in Marriage*. Grand Rapids, MI: Zondervan Publishing House.

CompCare Publishers. (1987). *Hope & Recovery: A Twelve Step Guide to Healing from Compulsive Sexual Behavior*. Minneapolis, MN: CompCare Publications.

Delitzsch, F. (n.d.). "Proverbs, Ecclesiastes, Song of Solomon." In C. F. Keil, & F. Delitzsch, *Commentary on the Old Testament* (J. Martin, Trans., Vol. 6). (Vol. 6). Grand Rapids, MI: William B. Eerdmans Publishing Company.

Dobson, J. (2001). *Bringing Up Boys*. Wheaton, IL: Tyndale House Publishers.

Earle, R., & Laaser, M. (2002). *The Pornography Trap: Setting Pastors and Laypersons Free from Sexual Addiction*. Kansas City, MO: Beacon Hill Press of Kansas City.

Eldredge, J. (2001). *Wild at Heart: Discovering the Secret of a Man's Soul*. Nashville, TN: Thomas Nelson Publishers.

Erickson, M. J. (1988). *Christian Theology*. Grand Rapids, MI: Baker Book House.

Findlay, G. G. (1970). "St. Paul's First Epistle to the Corinthians." In W. R. Nicoll (Ed.), *The Expositor's Greek Testament* (Vol. 2). Grand Rapids, MI: William B. Eerdmans Publishing Company.

Gangel, K. O. (1977). "Toward a Biblical Theology of Marriage and Family." *Journal of Psychology and Theology, 5* (1, 2, 3, & 4).

Glass, S. P. (2003). *Causes of Infidelity*. Retrieved July 21, 2005, from http://www.shirleyglass.com/reflect_infidelity4.htm.

Glass, S. P. (1998). *Shattered Vows: Getting Beyond Betrayal*. Retrieved July 21, 2005, from Smart Marriages: http://www.smartmarriages.com/glass.html.

Grudem, W. (2004). *Evangelical Feminism & Biblical Truth: An Analysis of More than 100 Disputed Questions*. Sisters, OR: Multnomah Publishers.

Hall, L. (1996). *An Affair of the Mind: One Woman's Courageous Battle to Salvage her Family from the Devastation of Pornography*. Wheaton, IL: Tyndale House.

Hauck, F. (1983). ἀμίαντος. In G. Kittel, & G. Friedrich (Eds.), *Theological Dictionary of the New Testament* (G. W. Bromiley, Trans., Vol. 4). Grand Rapids, MI: William B. Eerdmans Publishing Company.

Hauck, F., & Schulz, S. (1982). πόρνη, πόρνος, πορνεία, πορνεύω, ἐκπορνεύω. In G. Kittel, & G. Friedrich (Eds.), *Theological Dictionary of the New Testament* (G. W. Bromiley, Trans., Vol. 6). Grand Rapids, MI: William B. Eerdmans Publishing Company.

Henderson, D. (2005). *Think Before You Look*. Chattanooga, TN: AMG Publishers.

Hoekema, A. A. (1994). *Created in God's Image*. Grand Rapids, MI: William B. Eerdmans Publishing Company.

Hyde, J. S., & DeLamater, J. D. (2000). *Understanding Human Sexuality* (7th ed.). Madison, WI: McGraw-Hill Companies.

Internet Filter Review. (2007). *Internet Pornography Statistics*. Retrieved August 11, 2007, from http://www.internetfilterreview.com/internet-pornography-statistics.html.

Jayson, Sharon (2005, July 18). "Divorce Declining, but so is Marriage." *USA Today*. Retrieved July 23, 2008, http://www.usatoday.com/news/nation/2005-07-18-cohabit-divorce_x.htm.

Johnson, S. L. (1972). "The First Epistle to the Corinthians." In C. F. Pfeiffer, & E. F. Harrison (Eds.), *The Wycliffe Bible Commentary*. Chicago, IL: Moody Press.

Josephus, Flavius. (1981). *Josephus: Complete Works.* (William Whiston, Trans.). Grand Rapids, MI: Kregel Publications.

Keil, C. F., & Delitzsch, F. (n.d.). "The Pentateuch." In C. F. Keil, & F. Delitzsch, *Commentary on the Old Testament* (J. Martin, Trans., Vol. 1). Grand Rapids, MI: William B. Eerdmans Publishing Company.

Keil, C. F., & Delitzsch, F. (n.d.). "Joshua, Judges, Ruth, 1 & 2 Samuel." In C. F. Keil, & F. Delitzsch, *Commentary on the Old Testament* (J. Martin, Trans., Vol. 1). Grand Rapids, MI: William B. Eerdmans Publishing Company.

Kidner, D. (1972). "Genesis: An Introduction and Commentary." In D. J. Wiseman (Ed.), *The Tyndale Old Testament Commentaries.* Downers Grove, IL: InterVarsity Press.

Laaser, M. (1996). *Faithful & True: Sexual Integrity in a Fallen World.* Grand Rapids, MI: Zondervan Publishing House.

Laaser, M. (1996). *Faithful & True: Sexual Integrity in a Fallen World Workbook.* Nashville, TN: LifeWay Press.

Laaser, M. (1999). *Talking to Your Kids about Sex: How to Have a Lifetime of Age-Appropriate Conversations with Your Children about Healthy Sexuality.* Colorado Springs, CO: WaterBrook Press.

Laaser, M. (2001, January 16–19). *Treating the Addicted and Dysfunctional Family System.* Paper presented at Denver Seminary, Denver, CO.

Laaser, M. R. (2004). *Healing the Wounds of Sexual Addiction.* Grand Rapids, MI: Zondervan Publishing House.

Laumann, E. O., Gagnon, J. H., Michael, R. T., & Michaels, S. (1994). *The Social Organization of Sexuality: Sexual Practices in the United States.* Chicago, IL: University of Chicago Press.

Lewis, G. R., & Demarest, B. A. (1996). *Integrative Theology* (Vol. 2). Grand Rapids, MI: Zondervan Publishing House.

Lloyd-Jones, D. M. (1976). *Studies in the Sermon on the Mount.* Grand Rapids, MI: William B. Eerdmans Publishing Company.

Longman, T. I. (2004, July 28–30). *Biblical Exegesis and Marriage and Family Class Notes*. Paper presented at Denver Seminary, Denver, CO.

Longman, T. I. (2001). *Song of Songs*. Grand Rapids, MI: William B. Eerdmans Publishing Company.

MacArthur, J. (1985). *Matthew 1–7*. Chicago, IL: Moody Press.

Macrae, R. A. (2000). *The Effects of Premarital Heterosexual Behaviors on an Individual's Perspective of the Sexual Relationship in a Christian Marriage*. St. Paul, MN: Bethel Theological Seminary.

May, G. (1988). *Addiction & Grace: Love and Spirituality in the Healing of Addictions*. New York, NY: HarperCollins Publishers.

McLanahan, S. & Sandefur, G. (1994). *Growing Up with a Single Parent: What Hurts, What Helps*, Cambridge: Harvard University Press.

McFedries, P. (1996, July 25). *Starter Marriage*. Retrieved June 18, 2005, from http://www.wordspy.com/words/startermarriage.asp

McGaugh, J. L. (2003). *Making and Preserving Memories*. Retrieved July 20, 2005, from http://www.ihf.org/lecture/mcgaugh3_trans.html#top.

Merriam-Webster online dictionary. *Family.* Retrieved July 21, 2008, from http://www.merriam-webster.com/dictionary/family.

Milkman, H. B., & Sunderwirth, S. G. (1987). *Craving for Ecstasy: The Consciousness and Chemistry of Escape*. Lexington, MA: D. C. Heath and Company.

Minnery, T. (Ed.). (1986). *Pornography: A Human Tragedy*. Wheaton, IL: Tyndale House Publishers.

Mintle, L. S. (2005). *A New Trend: Starter Marriages*. Retrieved June 18, 2005, from http://www.cbn.com/LivingTheLife/Features/DrLindaHelps/StarterMarriages.asp.

Morris, L. (1975). *The First Epistle of Paul to the Corinthians*. In R. V. Tasker (Ed.), *Tyndale New Testament Commentaries* (Vol. 7). Grand Rapids, MI: William B. Eerdmans Publishing.

Moule, C. F. (1968). *An Idiom-Book of New Testament Greek*. London: Syndics of the Cambridge University Press.

Moulton, W. F., & Geden, A. S. (Eds.). (1963). *A Concordance to the Greek Testament*. Edinburgh, Scotland: T & T Clark.

Office of the General Assembly. (1983). *The Constitution of the Presbyterian Church (U.S.A.): Part 1, Book of Confessions*. New York, NY: The Office of the General Assembly.

Olds, J. (1956). "Pleasure Centers in the Brain." *Scientific American , 193*, 105–116.

Oliver, G. J. (2001, January 16–19). *Treating the Addicted and Dysfunctional Family System Class Notes*. Paper presented at Denver Seminary, Denver, CO.

Palmer, P. E. (1972). "Christian Marriage: Contract or Covenant?" *Theological Studies, 33* (4), 639.

Paul, P. (2005). *Pornified: How Pornography is Transforming our Lives, our Relationships, and our Families*. New York, NY: Times Books, Henry Holt and Company, LLC.

Paul, P. (2004, January 19). "The Porn Factor: In the Internet Age, Pornography is Almost Everywhere You Look. But What is it Doing to Real-Life Relationships?" *Time*, 163, 99.

Paul, P. (2003). *The Starter Marriage and the Future of Matrimony*. New York, NY: Random House Trade Paperbacks.

Pellauer, M. (1987). "Pornography: An Agenda for the Churches." *Christian Century, 104.22*, 651–655.

Piper, J. and Grudem, W. (1992). *50 Crucial Questions: An Overview of Central Concerns about Manhood and Womanhood.* Adapted from *Recovering Biblical Manhood and Womanhood.* Wheaton, IL: Crossway Books.

Plantinga, A. (1988). "Images of God." In M. Knoll, & D. Wells (Eds.), *Christian Faith and Practice in the Modern Practice in the Modern World.* Grand Rapids, MI: William B. Eerdmans Publishing Company.

Reisman, J. A. (2004, November 18). *Hearing on the Brain Science behind Pornography Addiction and the Effects of Addiction on Families and Communities.* Washington, DC: U. S. Senate Committee on Commerce, Science & Transportation.

Roberts, S. (2001, February 21). "Most Children Still Live in Two-Parent Homes, Census Bureau Reports." *The New York Times.* Retrieved August 3, 2008 from http://www.nytimes.com/2008/02/21/us/21census.html.

Robertson, A. T. (1931). *The Epistles of Paul* (Vol. 4). Nashville, TN: Broadman Press.

Rosenau, D. & Wilson, M. T. (2006). *Soul Virgins: Redefining Single Sexuality.* Grand Rapids, MI: Baker Books.

Ryrie, C. C. (1978). *The Ryrie Study Bible.* Chicago, IL: Moody Press.

Satinover, J. (2004, November 18). *Hearing on the Brain Science behind Pornography Addiction and the Effects of Addiction on Families and Communities.* Washington, DC: U. S. Senate Committee on Commerce, Science, and Transportation.

Schaeffer, F. (1972). *Genesis in Space and Time: The Flow of Biblical History.* Downers Grove, IL: InterVarsity Press.

Schaumberg, H. W. (1997). *False Intimacy: Understanding the Struggle of Sexual Addiction.* Colorado Springs, CO: NavPress.

Schaumberg, H. W. (2008). "False Intimacy and Sexual Addiction: A Modern Epidemic." *Christian Counseling Today, 15* (4), 25.

Schneider, J. (2000). "Effects of Cybersex Addiction on the Family: Results of a Survey." *Journal of Sexual Addiction & Compulsivity, 7,* 31–58.

Schneider, J. (2002). *The New 'Elephant in the Living Room': Effects of Compulsive Cybersex Behaviors on the Spouse.* In A. Cooper (Ed.), *Sex and the Internet: A Guide Book for Clinicians* (169–186). New York: Brunner-Routledge.

Schneider, J., Corley, D., & Irons, R. (1998). "Surviving Disclosure of Infidelity: Results of an International Survey of 164 Recovering Sex Addicts and Partners." *Journal of Sexual Addiction & Compulsivity, 5,* 189–217.

Scofield, C. I. (1945). *The Scofield Reference Bible.* New York, NY: Oxford University.

Skarnulis, L. (2003, July 14). *Is Solo Sex Hurting Your Relationship?* Retrieved January 24, 2004, from http://my.webmd.com/content/Article/70/81144.htm.

Smid, J. (1993). *Understanding Homosexuality.* Memphis, TN: Love In Action International, Inc.

Smith, L. P. (1953). *The Book of Ruth* (Vol. 2). Nashville, TN: Abingdom-Cokesbury Press.

Sproul, R. C. (1985). *The Holiness of God.* Wheaton, IL: Tyndale House Publishers, Inc.

Stanley, S., Trathen, D., McCain, S., Bryan, M. (1998). *A Lasting Promise: A Christian Guide to Fighting for Your Marriage.* San Francisco, CA: Jossey-Bass Publishers.

Storms, S. (2000). *Pleasures Evermore: The Life Changing Power of Enjoying God.* Colorado Springs, CO: NavPress.

Strong, A. H. (1972). *Systematic Theology.* Valley Forge, PA.: Judson Press.

Strong, J. (1970). *The Exhaustive Concordance of the Bible.* Nashville, TN: Abingdon Press.

Szuchman, L. T., & Muscarella, F. (Eds.). (2000). *Psychological Perspectives on Human Sexuality.* New York, NY: John Wiley & Sons, Inc.

Tasker, R. V. G. (1976). "The Gospel According to St. Matthew." In R. V. G. Tasker (Ed.), *Tyndale New Testament Commentaries.* Grand Rapids, MI: William B. Eerdmans Publishing Co.

The Barna Group. (2004, May 24). *Faith has a Limited Effect on Most People's Behavior.* Retrieved August 11, 2007, from The Barna Group: http://www.barna.org/FlexPage.aspx?Page=BarnaUpdate&B arnaUpdateID=164.

Thomas, G. (2000). *Sacred Marriage: What if God Designed Marriage to Make us Holy More than to Make us Happy.* Grand Rapids, MI: Zondervan Publishing House.

Thompson, A. P. (1983). "Extramarital Sex: A Review of the Research Literature." *The Journal of Sex Research, 19* (1), 1–22.

Unger, M. F. (1977). *Unger's Bible Dictionary.* Chicago, IL: Moody Press.

Veith, G. E. (2008, July 12/19). "Uncommon Bond: Family Collapse Opens a Door for Totalitarianism." *World, 23,* 29.

Veith, G. E. (2008, July 26/August 2). "Sex Appeal: How a Branch of Islam Wants to Convert the West." *World, 23, 29.*

Vine, W. E. (1981). *Vine's Expository Dictionary of Old and New Testament Words.* Old Tappan, NJ: Fleming H. Revell Co.

White, J. (1982). *Flirting with the World.* Wheaton, IL: Harold Shaw Publishers.

Wiersbe, W. (1989). *The Bible Exposition Commentary.* Wheaton, IL: Victor Books.

Woolf, I. A. (2008). *Purity Platoon Battle Plans.* Maple Grove, MN: National Coalition For Purity.

Woolf, I. A. (2008). *Purity Platoon Survey.* Maple Grove, MN: National Coalition For Purity.

Woolf, I. A. (2008). *Am I Sexually-Addicted? Assessment.* Maple Grove, MN: National Coalition For Purity.

About the Author
Dr. Irv Woolf
Director, National Coalition For Purity

Irv Woolf is a graduate of Bradley University (1969), Trinity
Evangelical Divinity School in Deerfield, Illinois, with a Master of Divinity
(1973), and Denver Seminary in Denver, Colorado, with a Doctor of Ministry
in Marriage and Family Counseling (2006). He is ordained in the Evangelical
Free Church of America (1995). Irv is an adjunct professor at the Association
of Free Lutheran Theological Seminary (AFLTS) and is the author of several
purity manuals including: *Purity Boot Camp Marching Orders, Purity Platoon
Battle Plans,* and *Maturity Platoon Combat Training Manual.* Having been a
pastor since 1973, Irv currently leads the National Coalition for Purity and the
popular men's purity ministry, Every Man's Battle For Purity. His passion is to
see the church, the Bride of Christ, become sexually pure and prepared for her
Bridegroom, Jesus Christ. Irv's wife, Elsie, is a Marriage and Family therapist.
Irv and Elsie are the parents of three adult children and seven beautiful
grandchildren. In his spare time, Irv enjoys golf, bicycling, and hot cider and
popcorn on a cold night. Irv and Elsie reside in Maple Grove, Minnesota.

Irv is available to speak at men's retreats, seminars, and conferences. Please

contact him at:

Dr. Irv Woolf

P. O. Box 631

Osseo, MN 55369

(612) 735-7359

ncfp@usfamily.net